Road Atlas of

Mercer County

New Jersey

Data Sources:

U.S. Census Bureau

U.S. Fish & Wildlife Service

U.S. Geological Survey

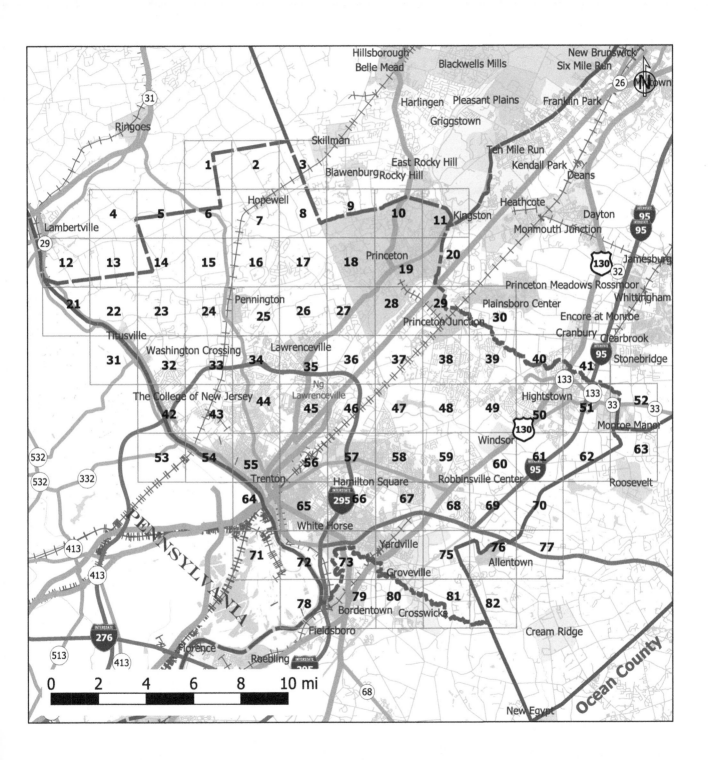

LEGEND

County Boundary		Cliff
Township Boundary		Dam/Levee
Municipal Boundary		Falls
Water		Harbor
Military Installation		Heliport
Native American Area		Hospital
Park		Mine
		Park
Interstate Highway		Post Office
		School
US Route		Spring
State Route		Summit
Local Road		Tower
Railway		Well
Airport		
Cemetery		
Church		

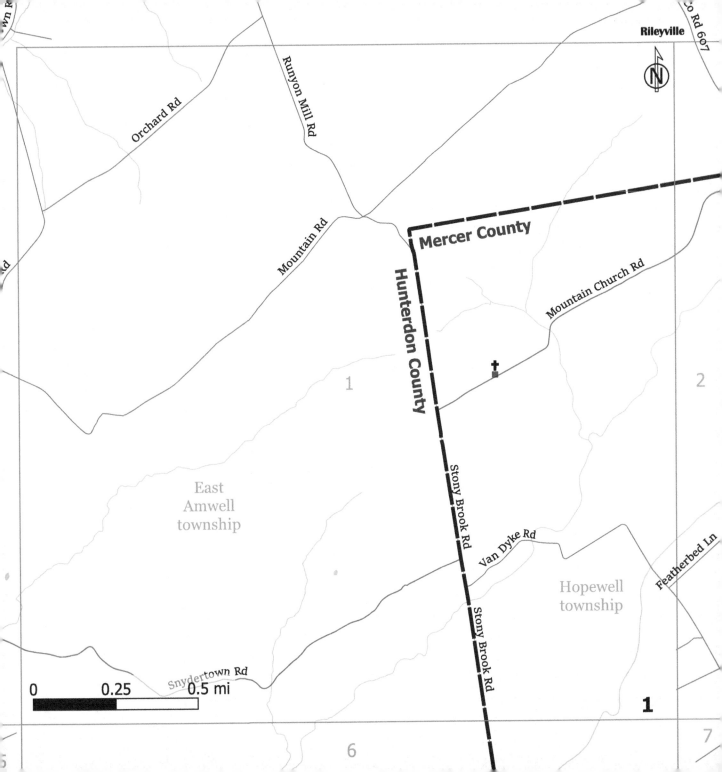

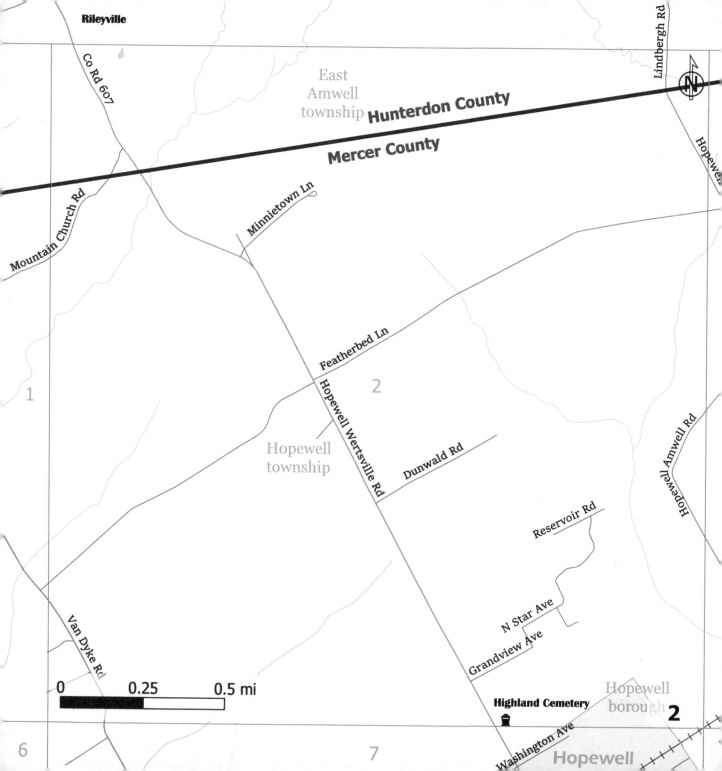

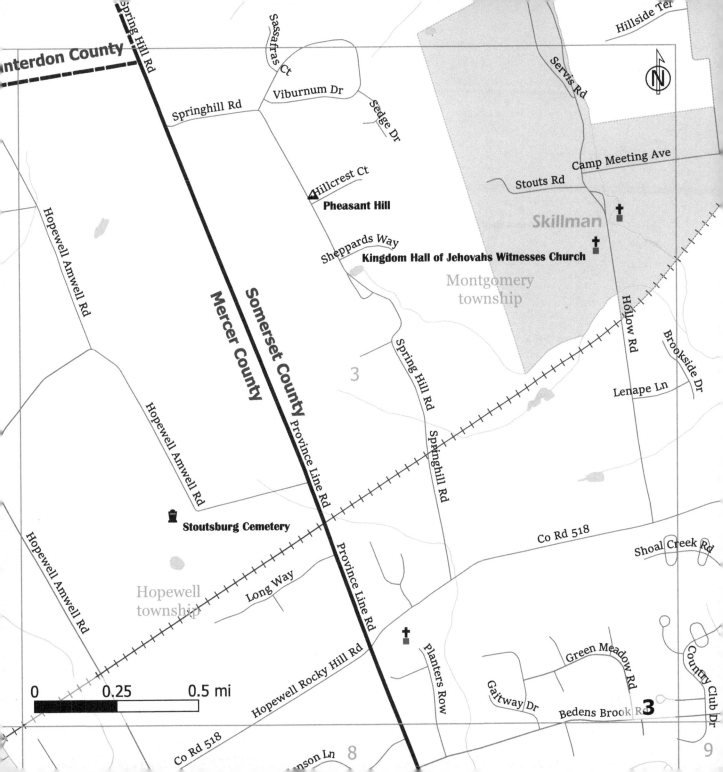

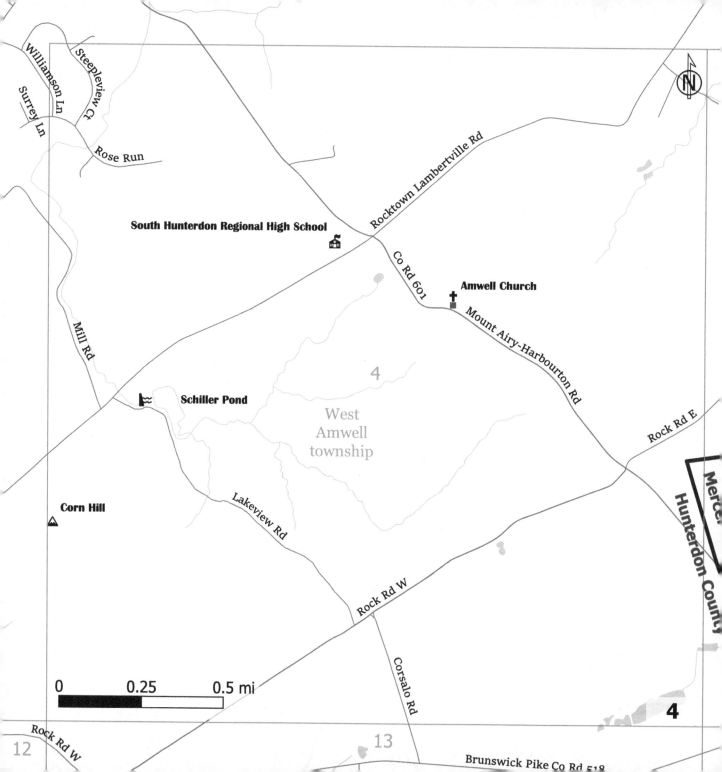

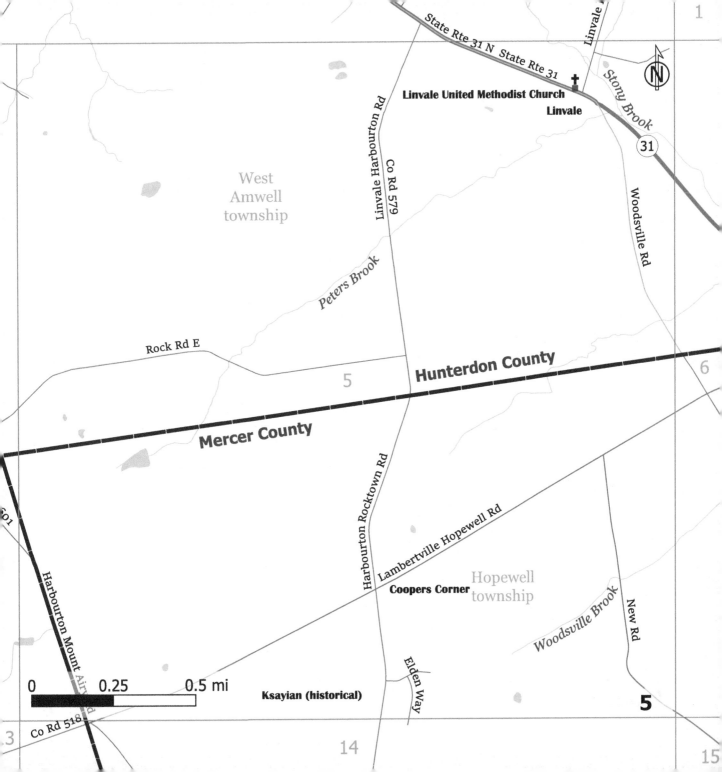

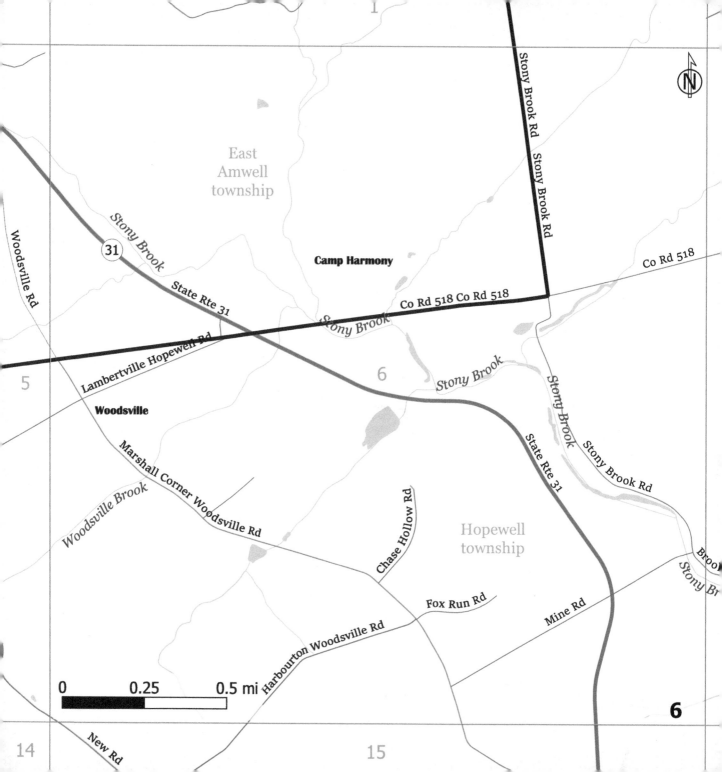

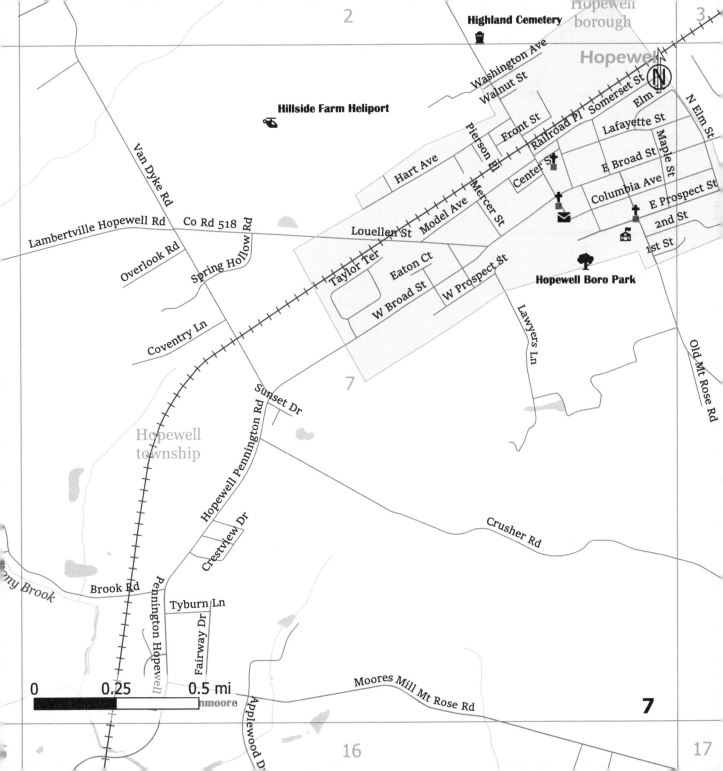

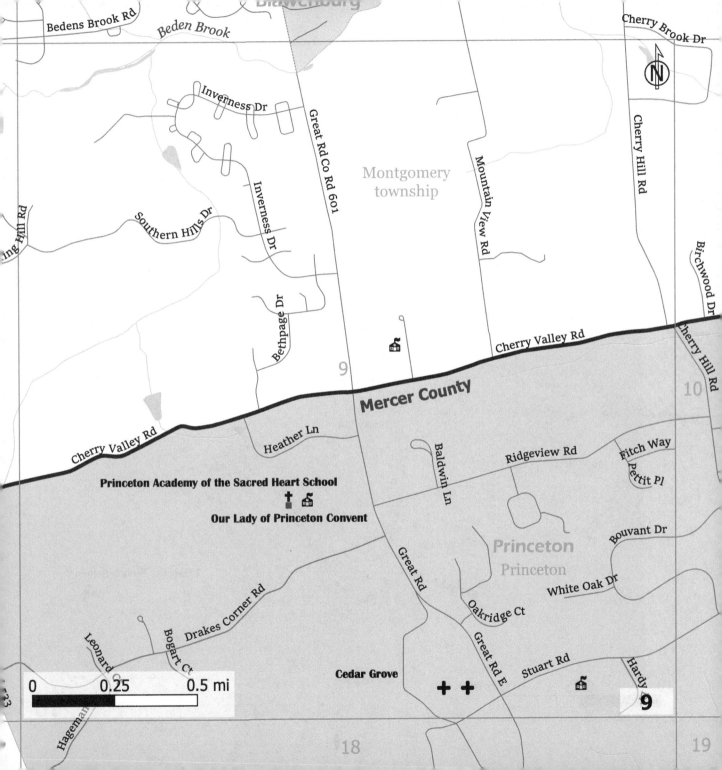

Bedens Brook Rd
Beden Brook
Cherry Brook Dr

Inverness Dr

Great Rd Co Rd 601

Cherry Hill Rd

ing Hill Rd

Inverness Dr

Montgomery township

Mountain View Rd

Birchwood Dr

Southern Hills Dr

Inverness Dr

Cherry Hill Rd

Bethpage Dr

Cherry Valley Rd

9

10

Mercer County

Cherry Valley Rd

Heather Ln

Baldwin Ln

Ridgeview Rd

Fitch Way

Pettit Pl

Princeton Academy of the Sacred Heart School

Our Lady of Princeton Convent

Bouvant Dr

Princeton
Princeton

Great Rd

White Oak Dr

Drakes Corner Rd

Oakridge Ct

Leonard

Bogart Ct

Great Rd E

Stuart Rd

Hardy

0   0.25   0.5 mi

Cedar Grove

9

Hageman

18

19

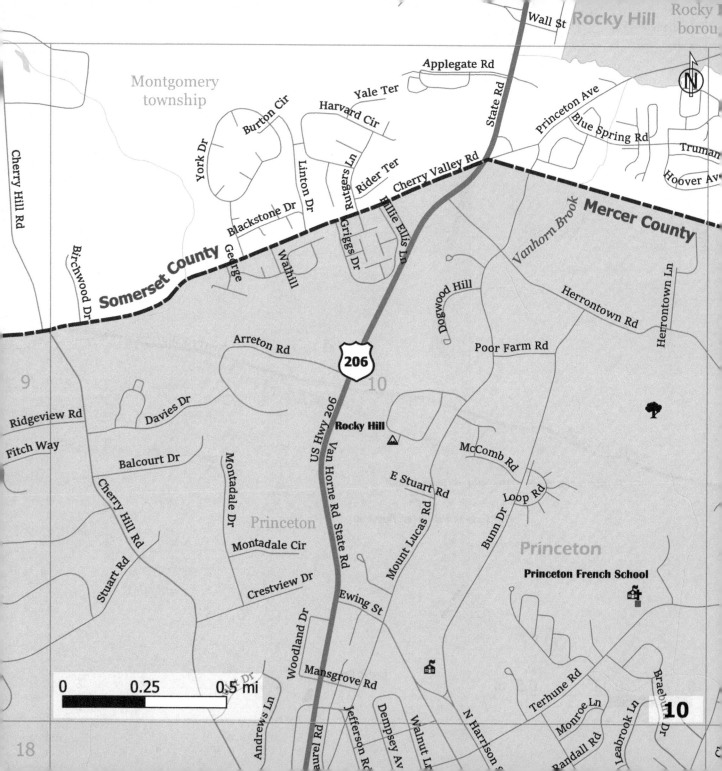

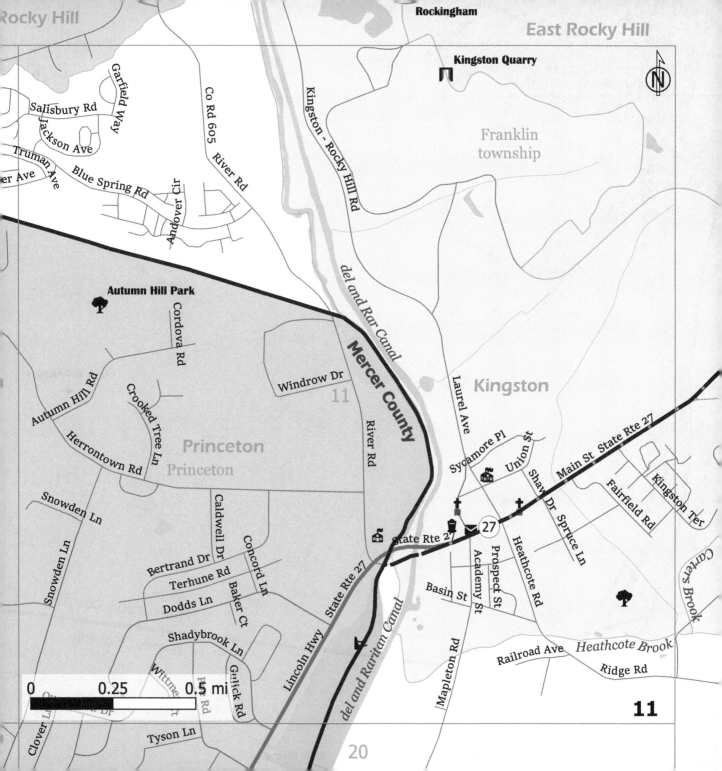

Rocky Hill

East Rocky Hill

Rockingham

Kingston Quarry

Franklin township

Salisbury Rd
Garfield Way
Jackson Ave
er Ave
Truman Ave
Blue Spring Rd
Andover Cir
Co Rd 605
River Rd

Kingston - Rocky Hill Rd

del and Rar Canal

Mercer County

Kingston

Autumn Hill Park

Cordova Rd

Windrow Dr

11

River Rd

Laurel Ave

Sycamore Pl
Union St
Main St State Rte 27
Fairfield Rd
Kingston Ter
Shaw Dr
Spruce Ln

Autumn Hill Rd
Crooked Tree Ln
Herrontown Rd

Princeton
Princeton

Snowden Ln
Snowden Ln

Caldwell Dr
Concord Ln
Bertrand Dr
Terhune Rd
Baker Ct
Dodds Ln

Shadybrook Ln
Gulick Rd
Wittme
Clover L
k Br
t Rd

Tyson Ln

State Rte 27
Lincoln Hwy
State Rte 27

27

State Rte 27

del and Raritan Canal

Basin St
Academy St
Mapleton Rd
Prospect St
Heathcote Rd

Railroad Ave
Heathcote Brook
Ridge Rd

Carters Brook

0   0.25   0.5 mi

11

20

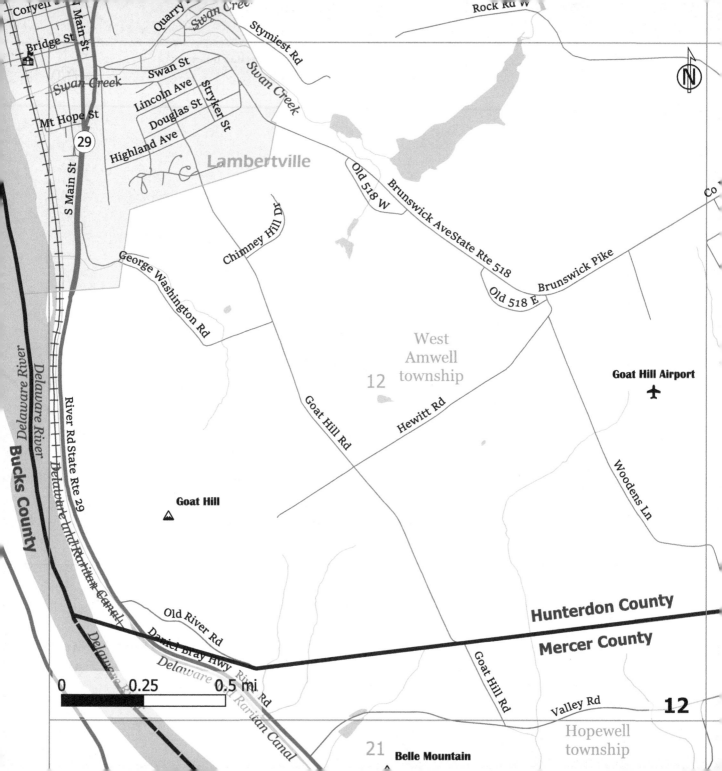

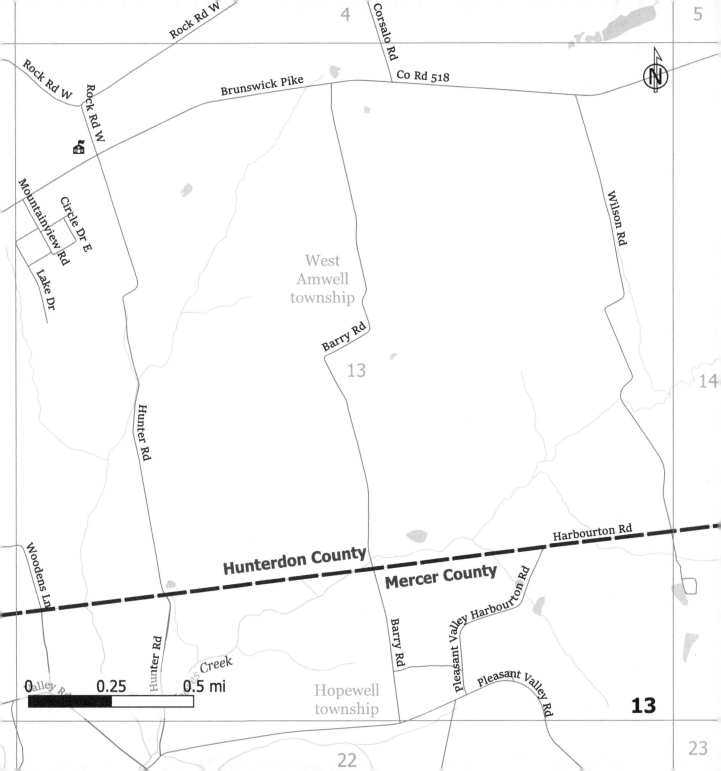

Rock Rd W

4

Corsalo Rd

5

Rock Rd W

Rock Rd W

Brunswick Pike

Co Rd 518

N

Mountainview Rd

Circle Dr E

West
Amwell
township

Wilson Rd

Lake Dr

Barry Rd

13

14

Hunter Rd

Harbourton Rd

Woodens Ln

Hunterdon County

Mercer County

Pleasant Valley Harbourton Rd

Barry Rd

0   0.25   0.5 mi

Hunter Rd

Valley Rd

Creek

Pleasant Valley Rd

Hopewell
township

13

22

23

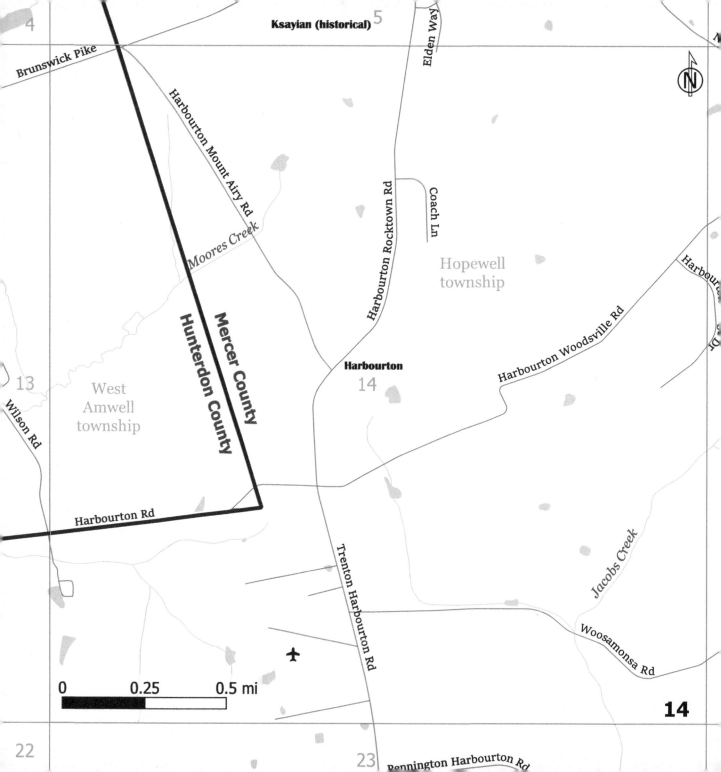

4

Ksayian (historical) 5

Elden Way

N

Brunswick Pike

Harbourton Mount Airy Rd

Moores Creek

Harbourton Rocktown Rd

Coach Ln

Hopewell township

Harbourton

Harbourt...

Mercer County

Hunterdon County

Harbourton Woodsville Rd

13

West Amwell township

Wilson Rd

Harbourton

14

Harbourton Rd

Jacobs Creek

Trenton Harbourton Rd

Woosamonsa Rd

0   0.25   0.5 mi

14

22

23 Pennington Harbourton Rd

New Rd

Harbourton Woodsville Rd

Marshall Corner Woodsville Rd

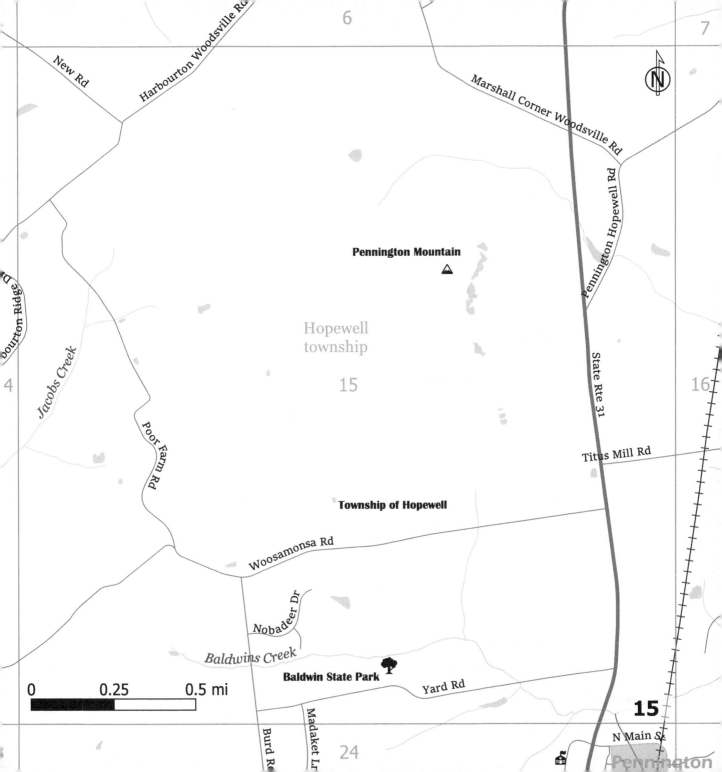

N

Pennington Hopewell Rd

bourton Ridge D

Jacobs Creek

Pennington Mountain

Hopewell
township

15

State Rte 31

Poor Farm Rd

Titus Mill Rd

Township of Hopewell

Woosamonsa Rd

Nobadeer Dr

Baldwins Creek

Baldwin State Park

Yard Rd

Burd Rd

Madaket Ln

24

15

N Main St

Pennington

| 0 | 0.25 | 0.5 mi |

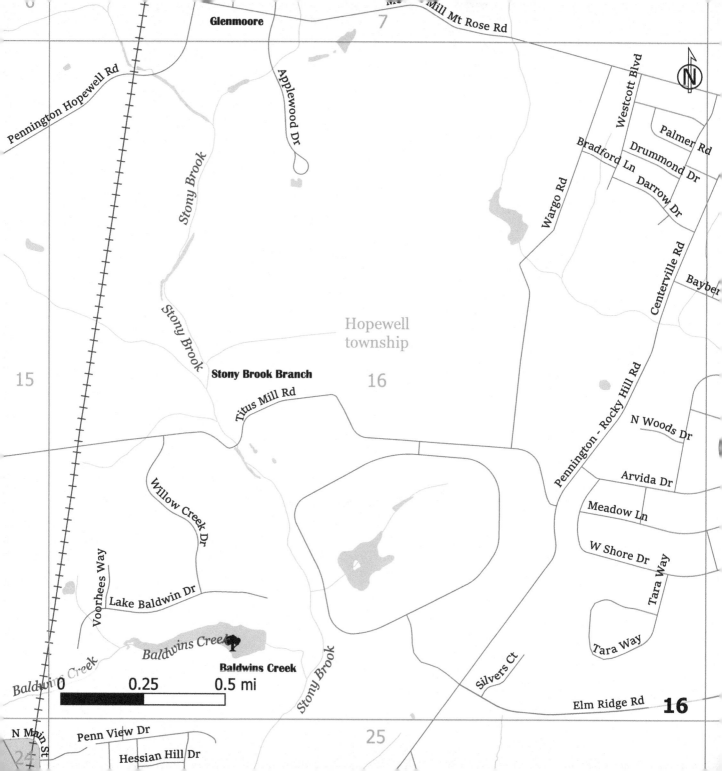

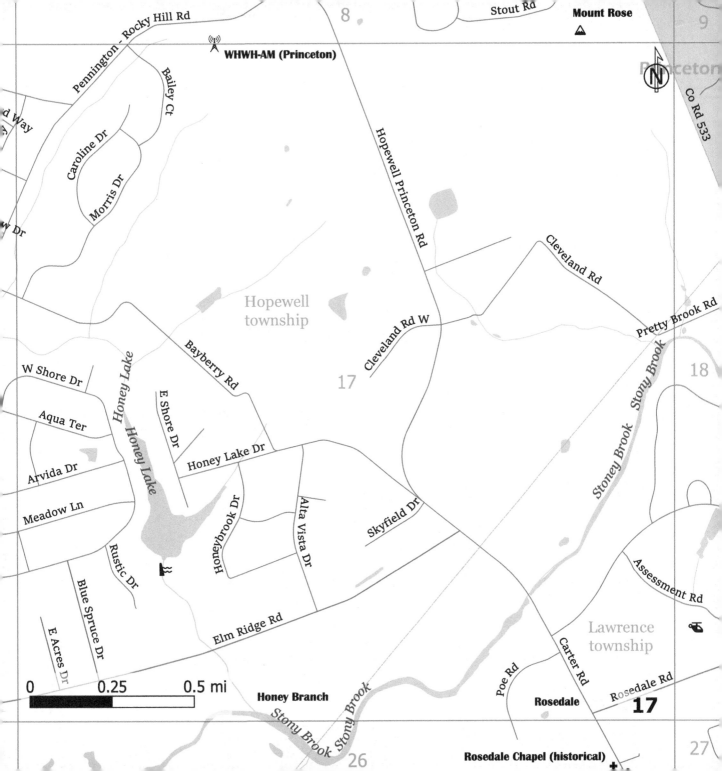

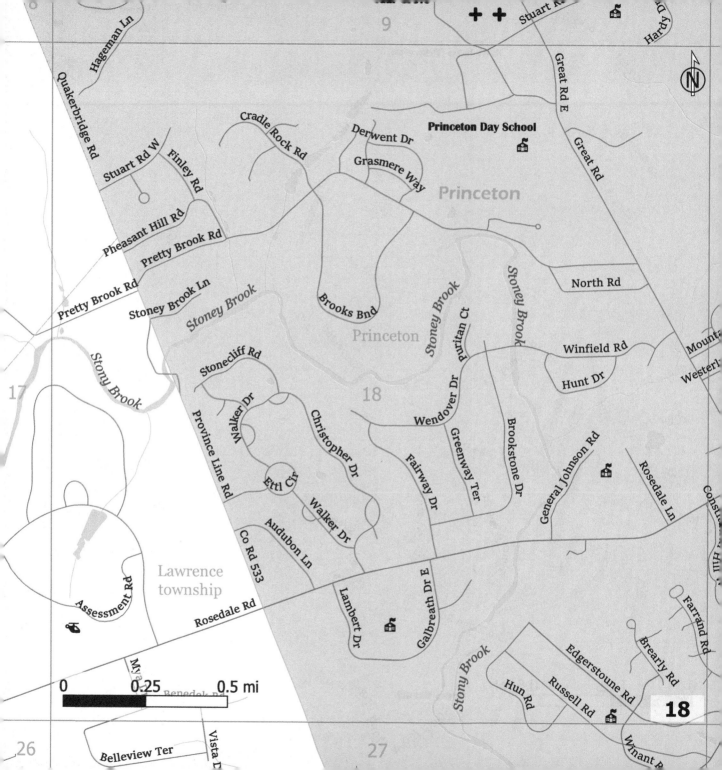

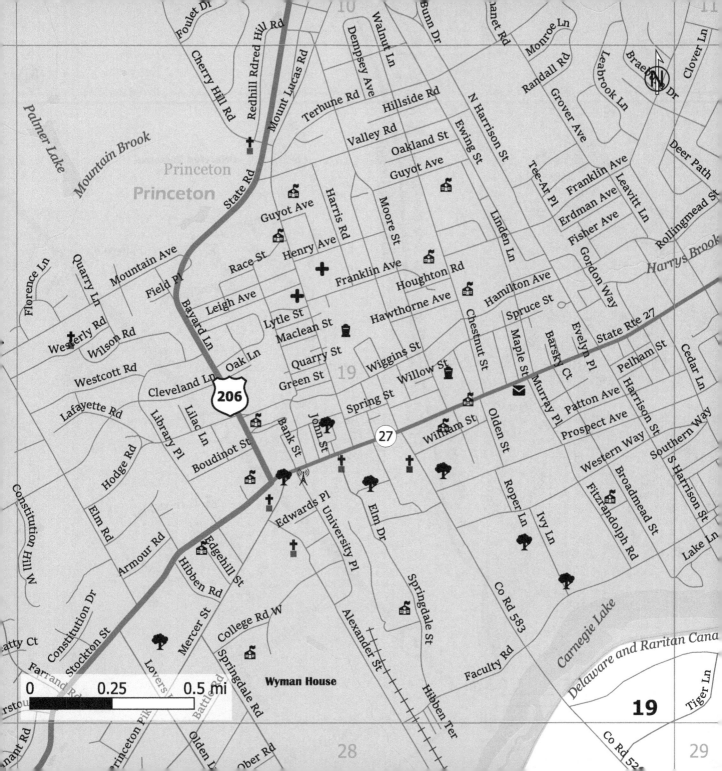

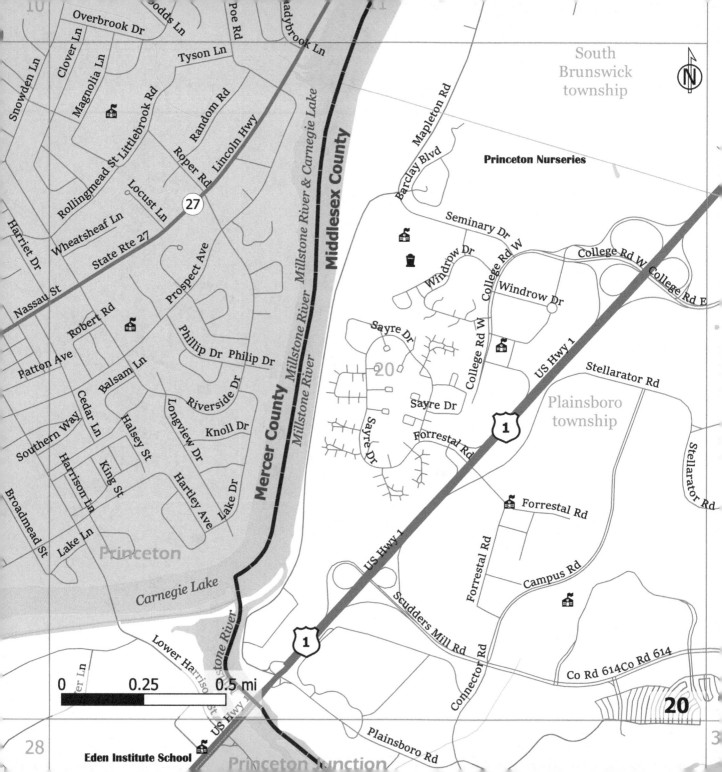

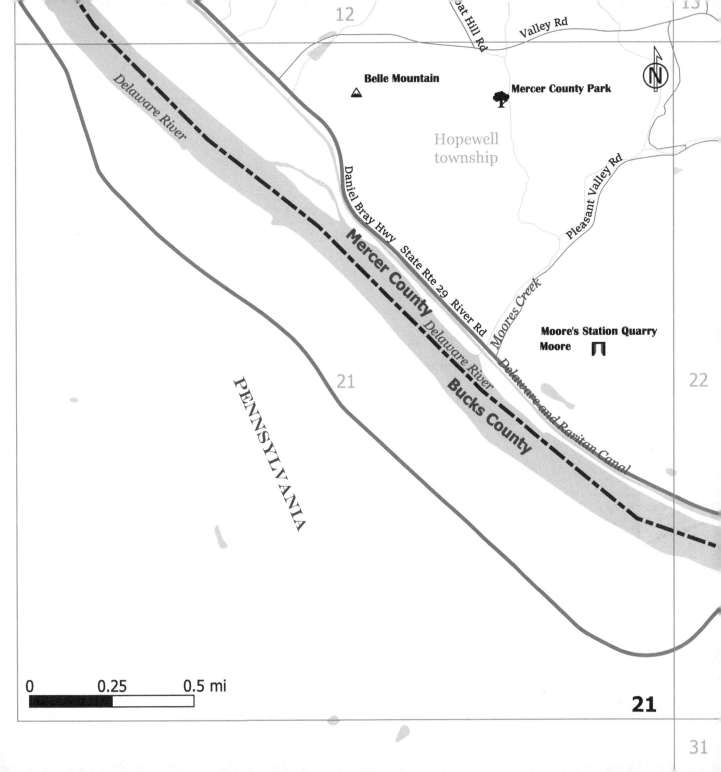

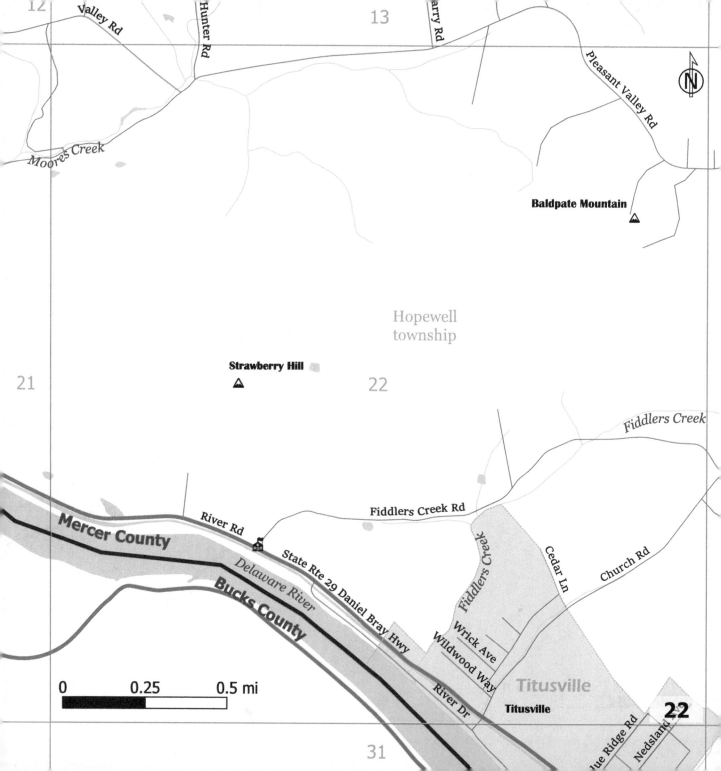

12

Valley Rd

Hunter Rd

13

arry Rd

Pleasant Valley Rd

N

Moores Creek

Baldpate Mountain
△

Hopewell township

Strawberry Hill
△

21

22

Fiddlers Creek

Fiddlers Creek Rd

River Rd

Fiddlers Creek

Mercer County

State Rte 29 Daniel Bray Hwy

Cedar Ln

Church Rd

Delaware River

Bucks County

Wrick Ave

Wildwood Way

Titusville

River Dr

Titusville

0   0.25   0.5 mi

lue Ridge Rd

Nedsland

22

31

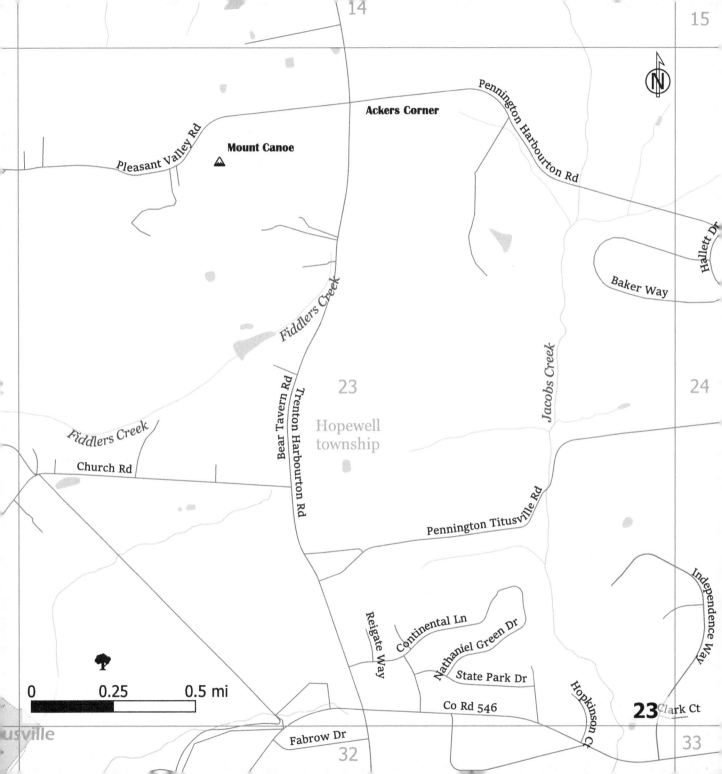

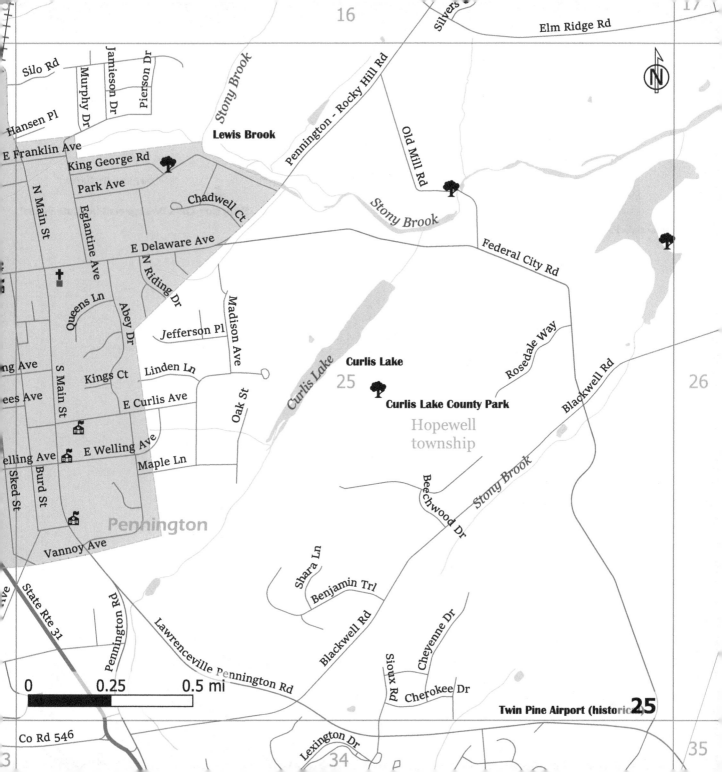

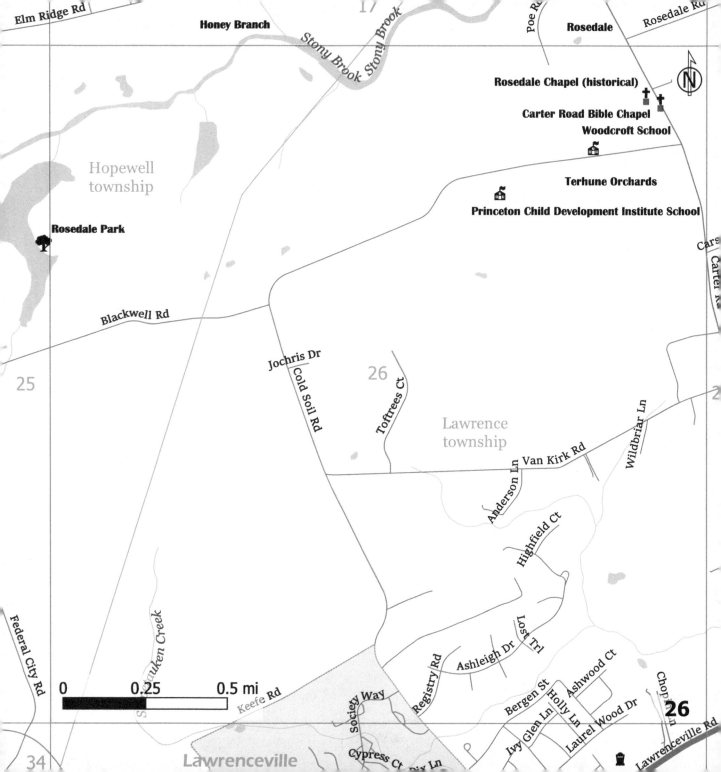

Elm Ridge Rd

Honey Branch

Stony Brook Stony Brook

Poe Rd

Rosedale

Rosedale Rd

Rosedale Rd

N

Rosedale Chapel (historical)

Carter Road Bible Chapel

Woodcroft School

Hopewell township

Terhune Orchards

Princeton Child Development Institute School

Rosedale Park

Cars

Carter Rd

Blackwell Rd

Jochris Dr

26

25

Cold Soil Rd

Toftrees Ct

Lawrence township

Wildbriar Ln

2

Anderson Ln   Van Kirk Rd

Highfield Ct

Federal City Rd

S Mecaukin Creek

Lost Trl

Ashwood Ct

Registry Rd

Ashleigh Dr

Chop Ln

0   0.25   0.5 mi

Keefe Rd

Society Way

Bergen St

Holly Ln

Ivy Glen Ln

Ashwood Ct

Laurel Wood Dr

26

34

Cypress Ct

Div Ln

Lawrenceville

Lawrenceville Rd

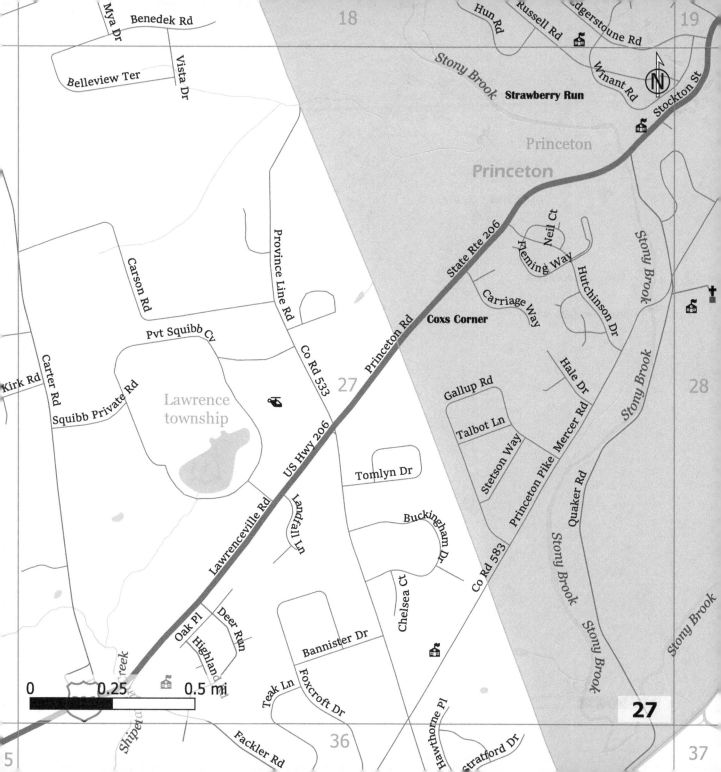

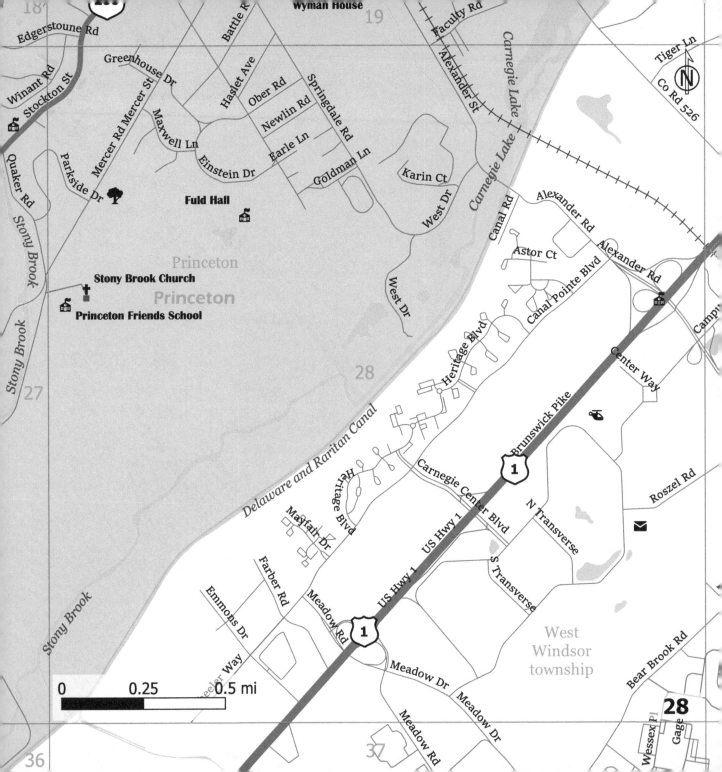

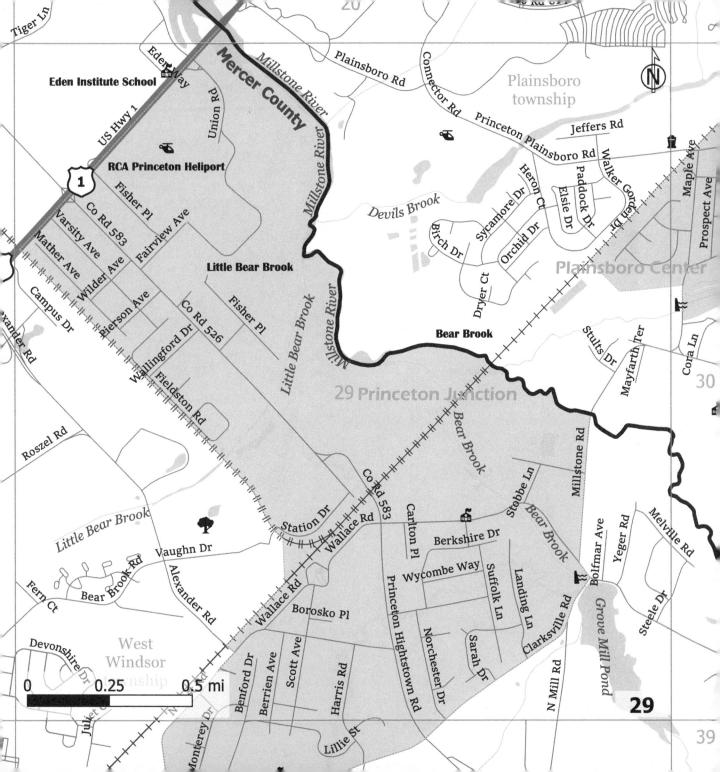

Tiger Ln

Eden Institute School

Eden Way

Millstone River

Mercer County

20

Plainsboro Rd

Connector Rd

Plainsboro township

N

US Hwy 1

Union Rd

Princeton Plainsboro Rd

Jeffers Rd

Walker Gordon Dr

Maple Ave

Prospect Ave

1

RCA Princeton Heliport

Fisher Pl

Fairview Ave

Co Rd 583

Varsity Ave

Wilder Ave

Millstone River

Devils Brook

Heron Ct

Sycamore Dr

Paddock Dr

Elsie Dr

Little Bear Brook

Birch Dr

Orchid Dr

Plainsboro Center

Mather Ave

Pierson Ave

Co Rd 526

Fisher Pl

Little Bear Brook

Millstone River

Dryer Ct

Campus Dr

Wallingford Dr

Fieldston Rd

Bear Brook

Stults Dr

Mayfarth Ter

Cora Ln

30

Alexander Rd

29 Princeton Junction

Bear Brook

Roszel Rd

Millstone Rd

Co Rd 583

Stobbe Ln

Bear Brook

Little Bear Brook

Station Dr

Wallace Rd

Carlton Pl

Berkshire Dr

Bolfmar Ave

Yeger Rd

Melville Rd

Vaughn Dr

Wycombe Way

Suffolk Ln

Landing Ln

Clarksville Rd

Grove Mill Pond

Steele Dr

Fern Ct

Bear Brook Rd

Alexander Rd

Wallace Rd

Borosko Pl

Princeton Hightstown Rd

Sarah Dr

N Mill Rd

Devonshire Dr

West Windsor Township

Benford Dr

Berrien Ave

Scott Ave

Harris Rd

Norchester Dr

29

Juliet Ct

Monterey Dr

Lillie St

39

0   0.25   0.5 mi

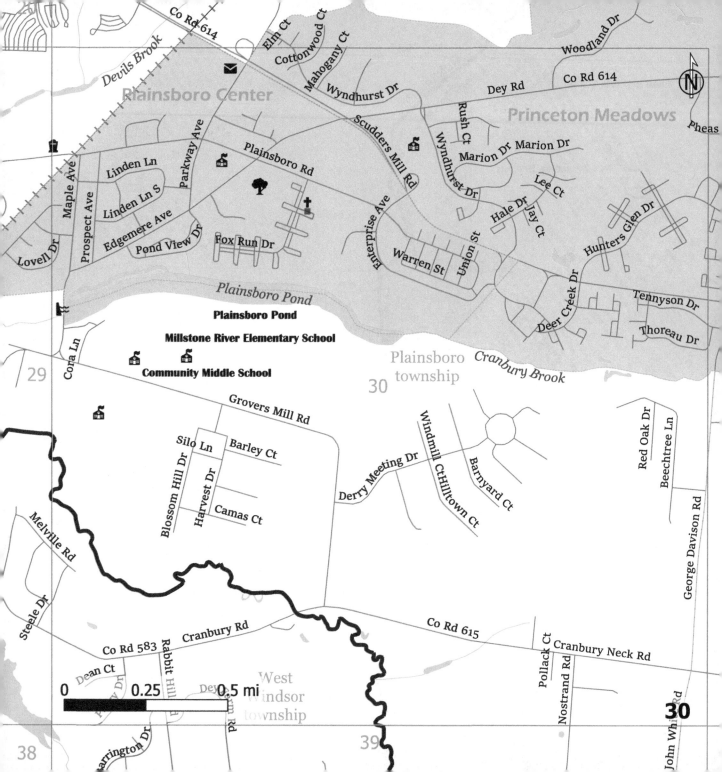

River Rd

Titusville

Titusville

State Rte 29

Nedsland Ave

Park Lake Ave

River Dr

Grant St

Delaware River

Bucks County

Mercer County

River Dr

PENNSYLVANIA

532

0   0.25   0.5 mi

31

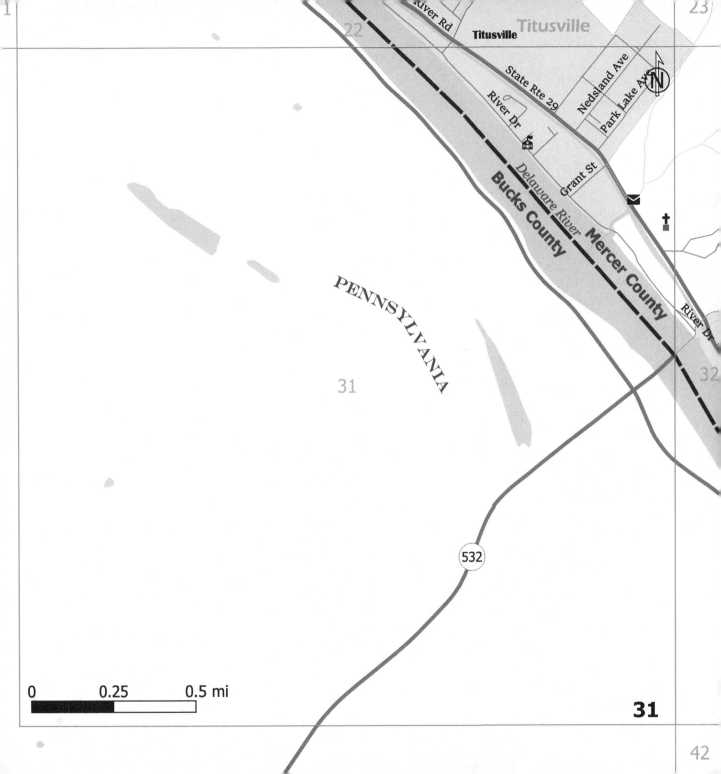

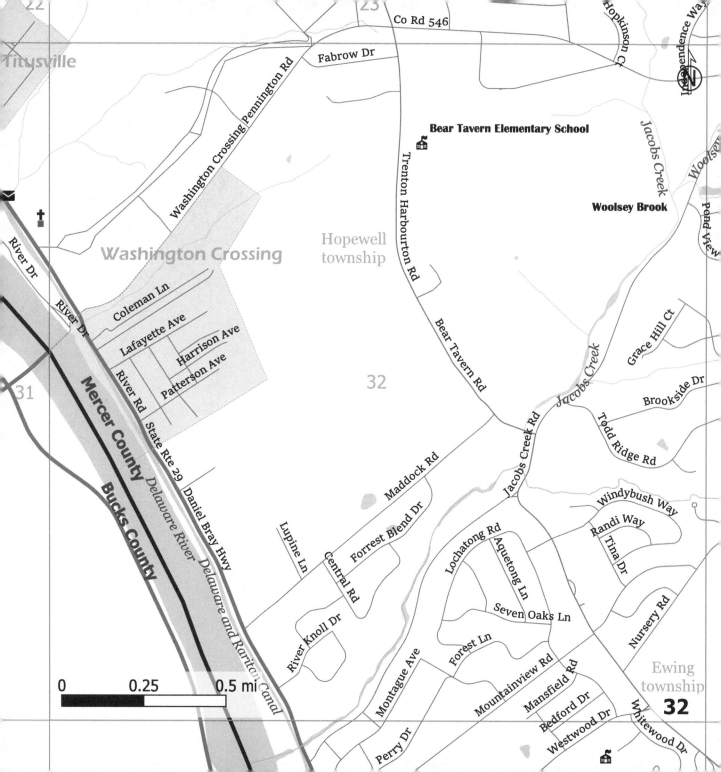

22

23

Co Rd 546

Titusville

Fabrow Dr

Hopkinson Ct

Independence Way

N

Washington Crossing Pennington Rd

Bear Tavern Elementary School

Jacobs Creek

Woolsey

Trenton Harbourton Rd

Woolsey Brook

Pond View

Hopewell township

Washington Crossing

River Dr

Coleman Ln

Lafayette Ave

Harrison Ave

Patterson Ave

Bear Tavern Rd

32

Grace Hill Ct

River Dr

River Rd

31

State Rte 29

Jacobs Creek

Jacobs Creek Rd

Jacobs Creek

Brookside Dr

Mercer County

Daniel Bray Hwy

Todd Ridge Rd

Bucks County

Delaware River

Maddock Rd

Windybush Way

Delaware and Raritan Canal

Lupine Ln

Forrest Blend Dr

Central Rd

Lochatong Rd

Aquetong Ln

Randi Way

Tina Dr

Nursery Rd

River Knoll Dr

Seven Oaks Ln

0   0.25   0.5 mi

Montague Ave

Forest Ln

Mountainview Rd

Mansfield Rd

Ewing township

32

Perry Dr

Bedford Dr

Westwood Dr

Whitewood Dr

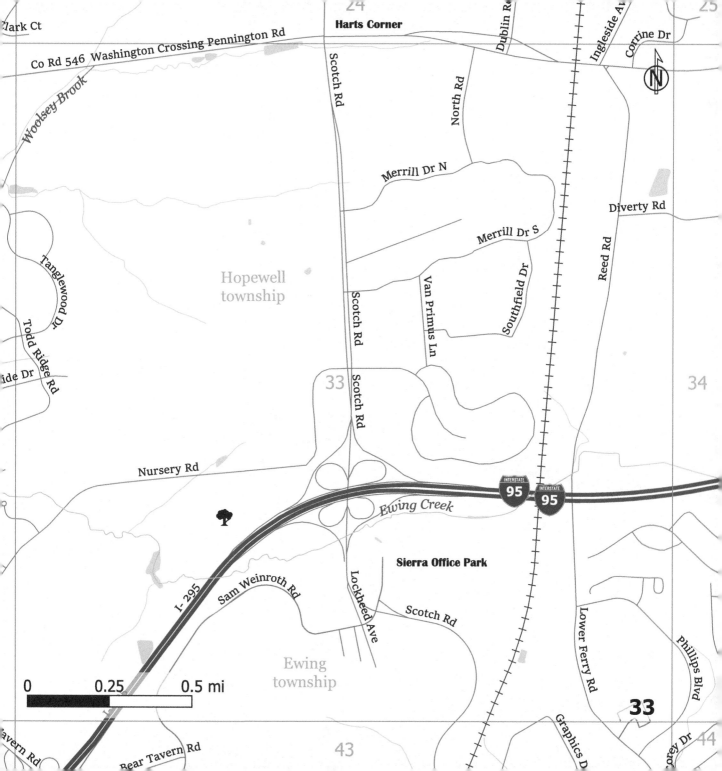

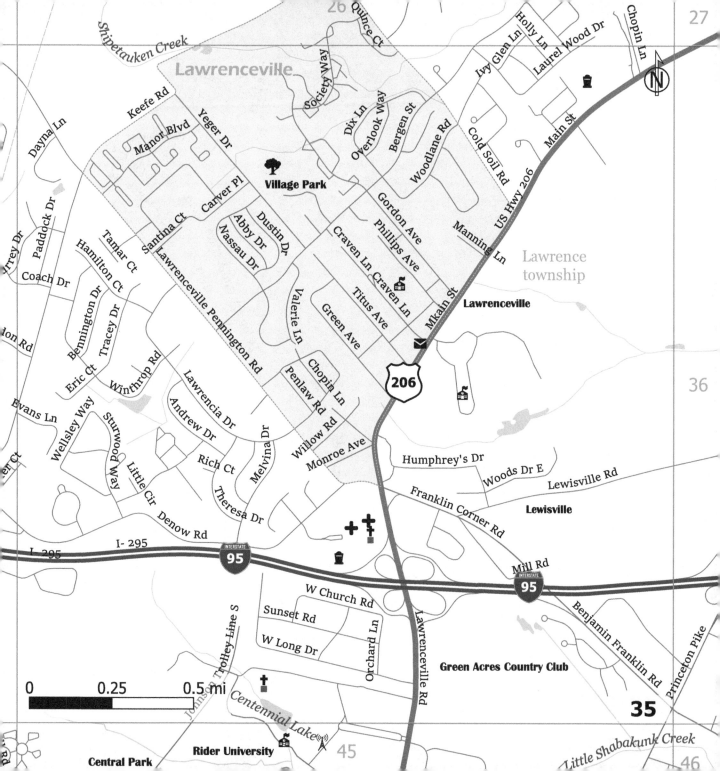

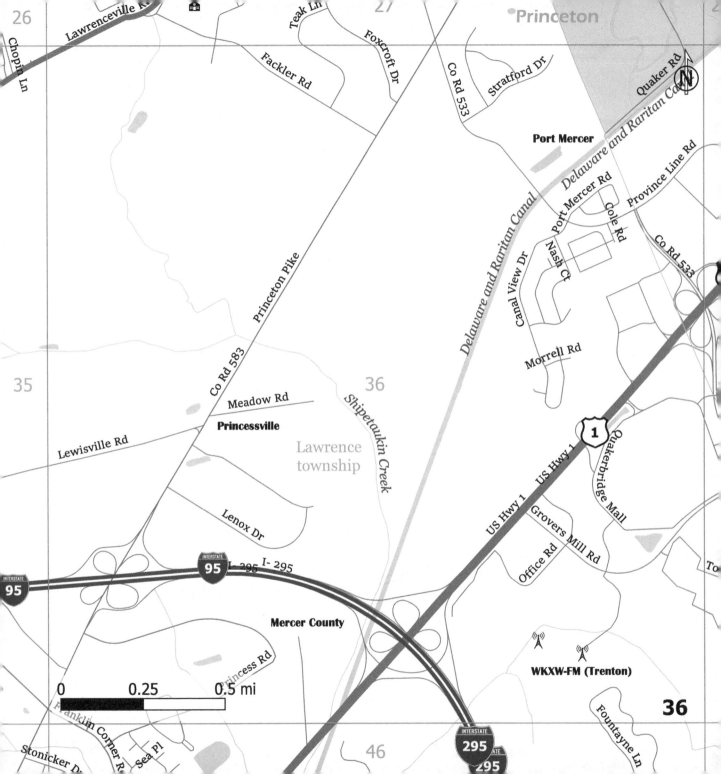

26

Chopin Ln

Lawrenceville Rd

Teak Ln

27

Princeton

Fackler Rd

Foxcroft Dr

Co Rd 553

Stratford Dr

Quaker Rd

N

Delaware and Raritan Canal

Port Mercer

Port Mercer Rd

Province Line Rd

Cole Rd

Co Rd 533

Canal View Dr

Nash Ct

Delaware and Raritan Canal

Morrell Rd

Princeton Pike

Co Rd 583

35

36

Meadow Rd

Shipetaukin Creek

Princessville

Lawrence
township

Lewisville Rd

US Hwy 1

US Hwy 1

1

Quakerbridge Mall

Lenox Dr

US Hwy 1

Grovers Mill Rd

INTERSTATE
95

I- 295

I- 295

Office Rd

INTERSTATE
95

Mercer County

To

WKXW-FM (Trenton)

Princess Rd

0   0.25   0.5 mi

36

Franklin Corner Rd

Fountayne Ln

Stonicker Dr

Sea Pl

46

INTERSTATE
295

INTERSTATE
295

Princeton

Wheeler Wa...

US Hwy 1

Brunswick Pike

Province Line Rd

Meadow Dr

Bear Brook Rd

Wessex Pl

Wessex Pl

Gage Pl

Wessex Dr

N

Upper Bear Swamp

Ascot Cres

Caleb Ln

Renfield Dr

Meadow Rd

West
Windsor
township

Heather Dr

West Windsor Commerce Center

Windsor Dr

Clarksville Rd

37

38

Raven Blvd

Rookery Ct

Jacob Dr

Co Rd 533

American Cyanamid Helistop

✈

Victoria Pl

Springhill Dr

Haskel Dr

Edith Ct

...rs Mill Rd

Jamieson Dr

Zeloof Dr

Ann's Ct

Lake Shore Dr

PSE and G Trenton Distribution Helistop

✈

Stafford Dr

Windsor Pond Rd

Warwick Rd

Deerfield Dr

Deerfield Dr

Woodhollow Rd

Greene Ct

Greene Dr

Town Ct N

Quakerbridge Rd   Co Rd 533

York Rd

S Post Rd

0   0.25   0.5 mi

Cedar Dr

...alm St

✝

Village Rd W

S Post Rd

47

37

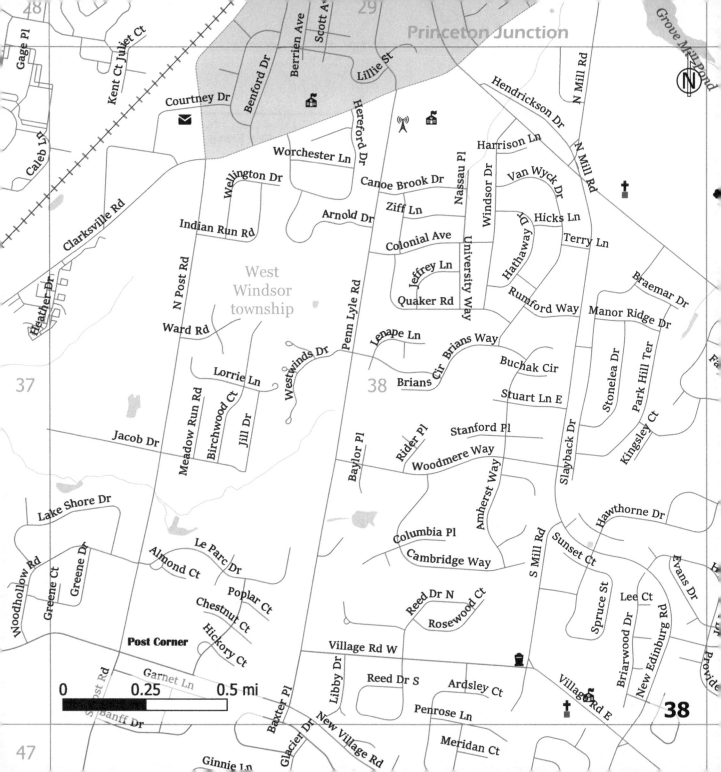

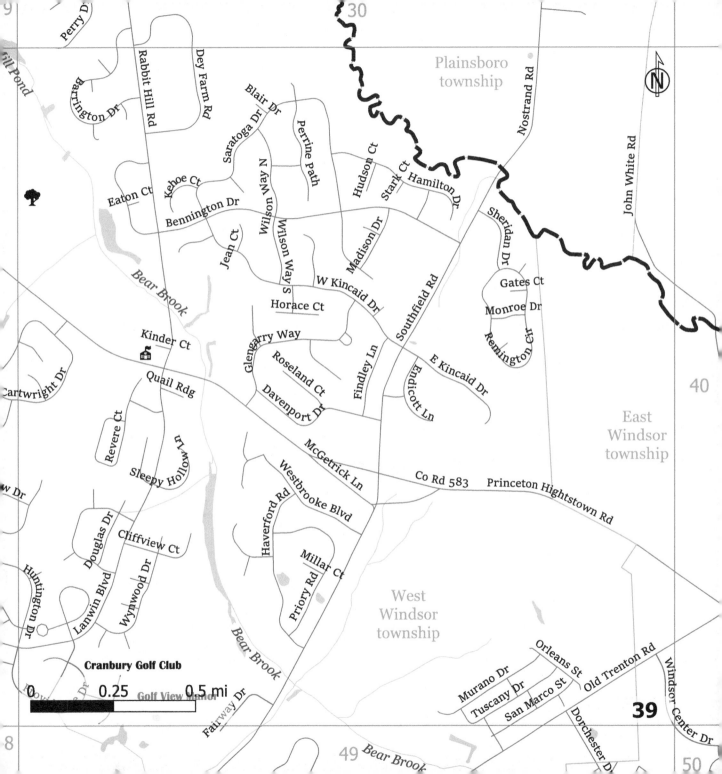

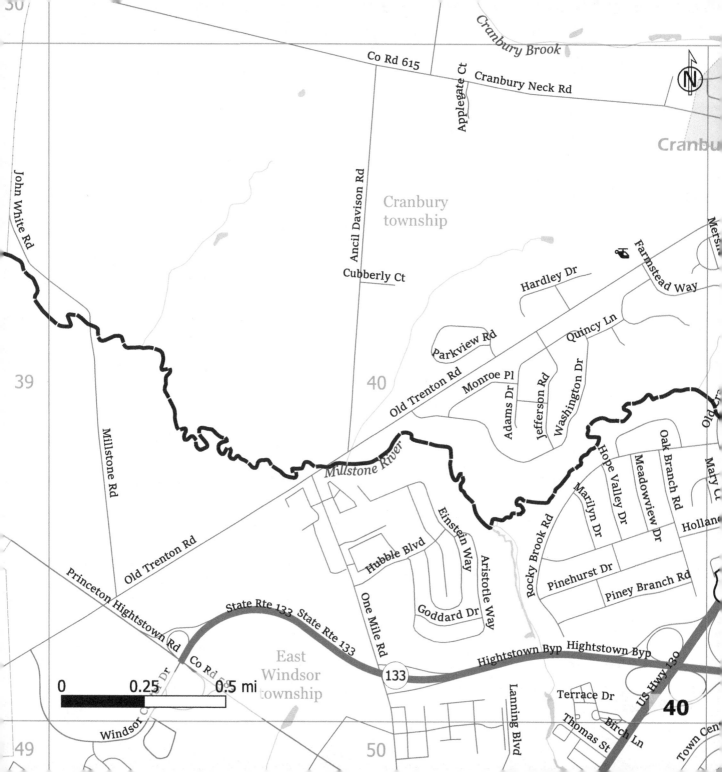

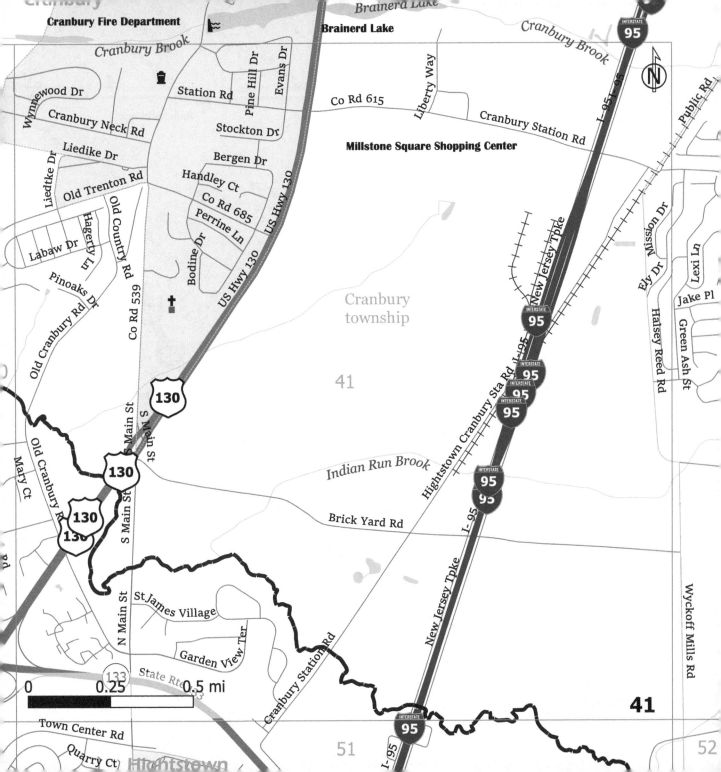

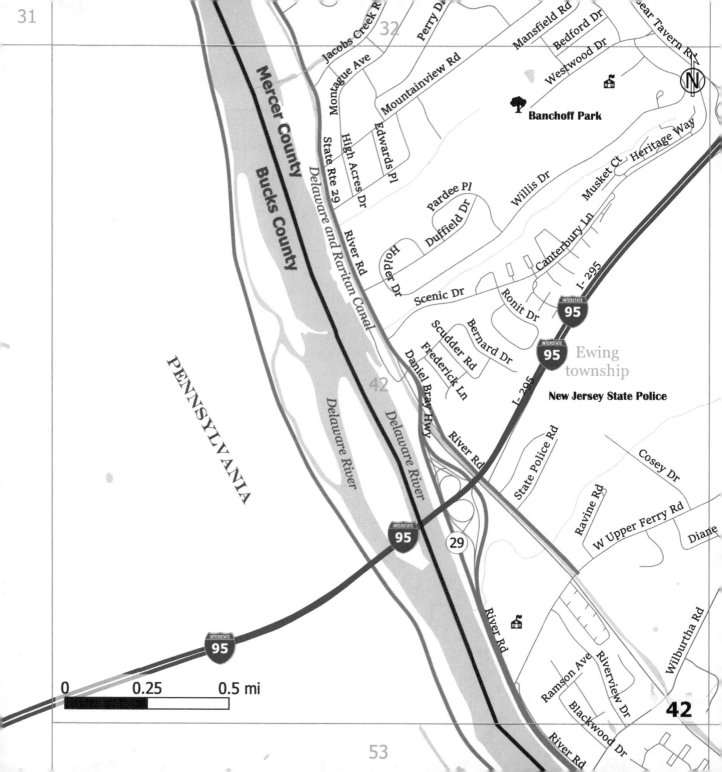

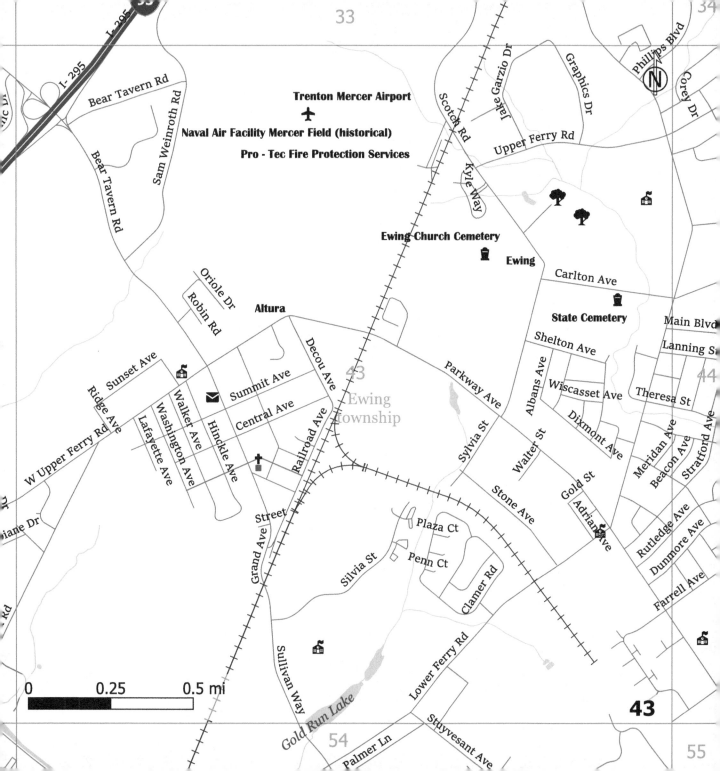

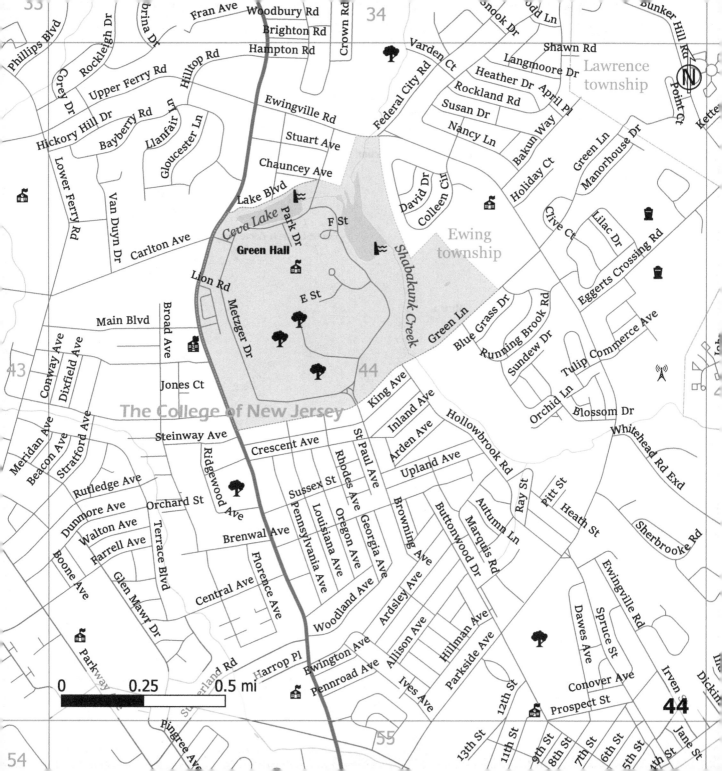

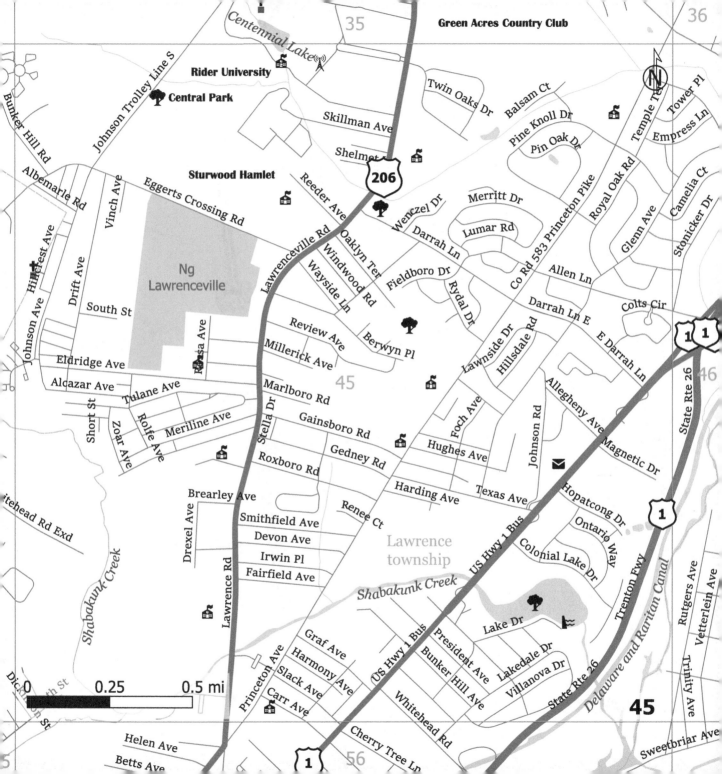

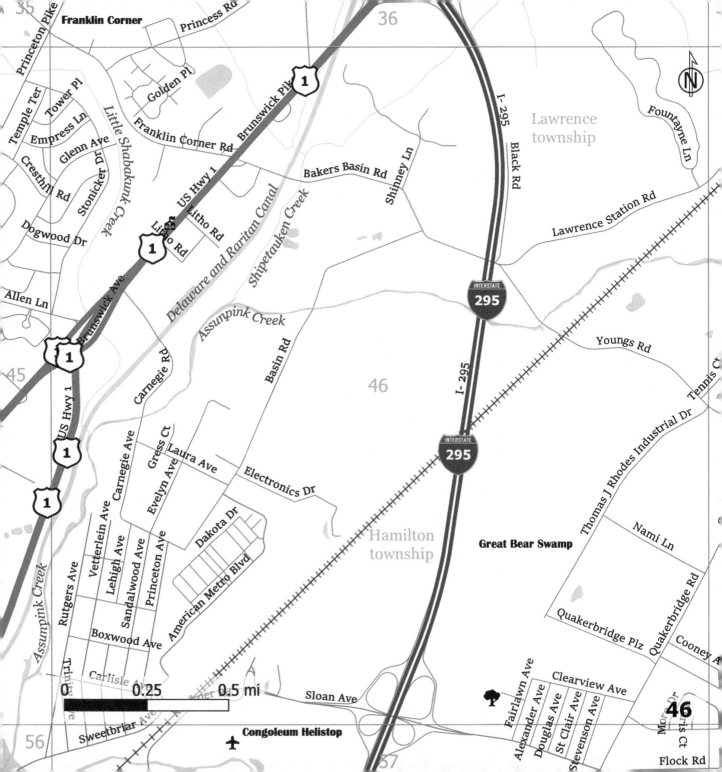

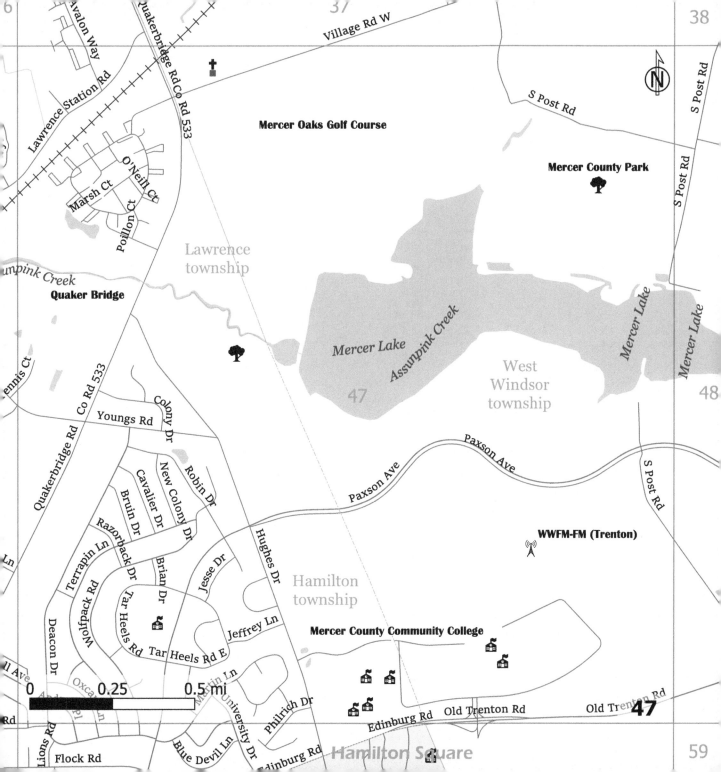

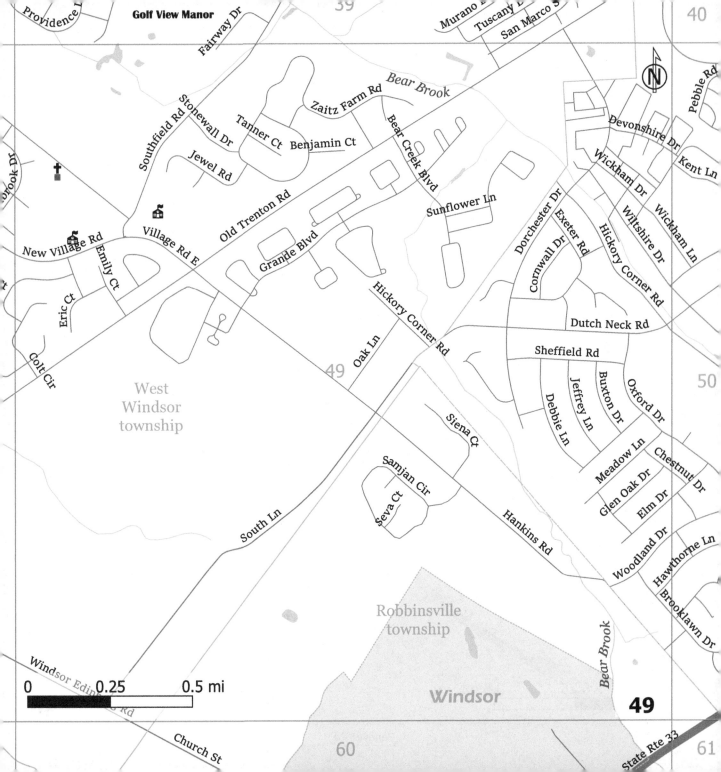

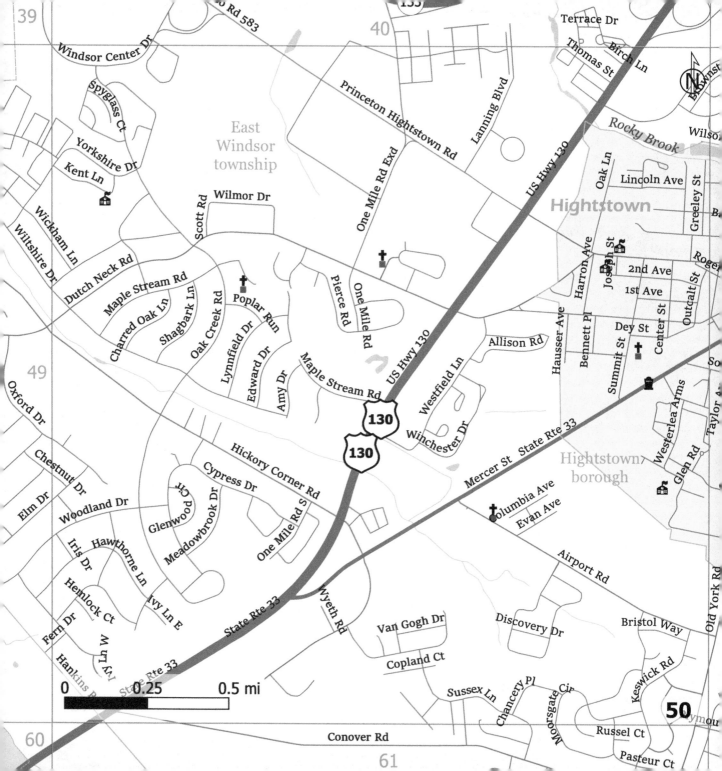

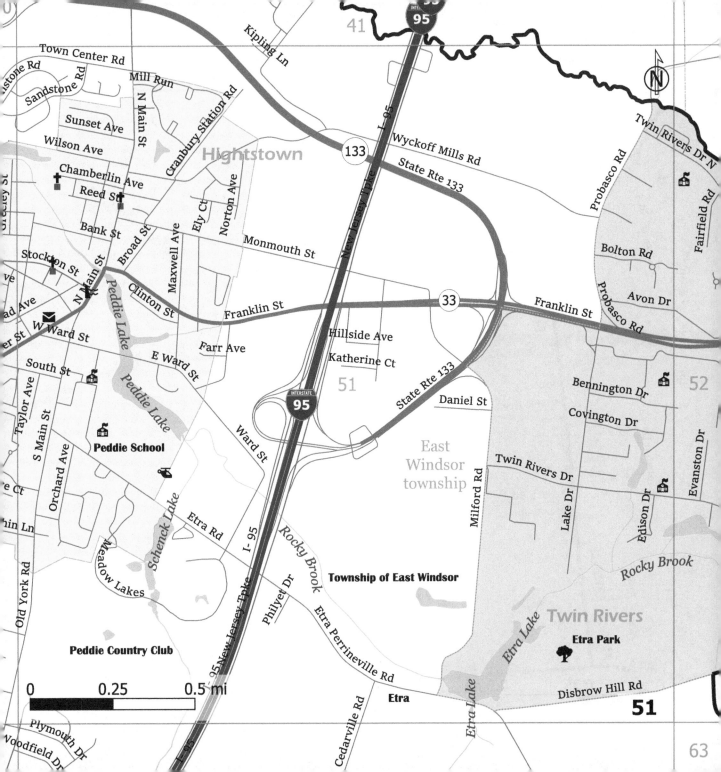

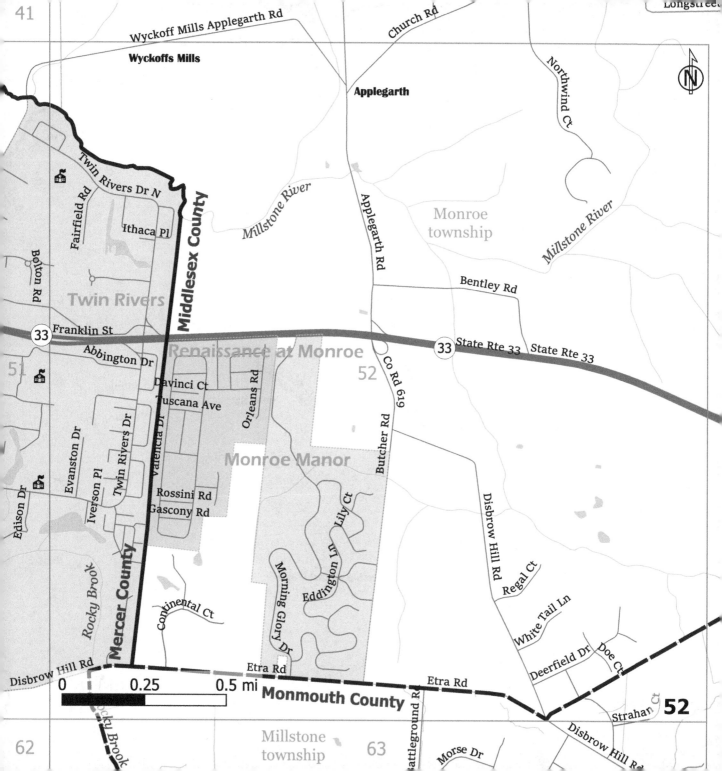

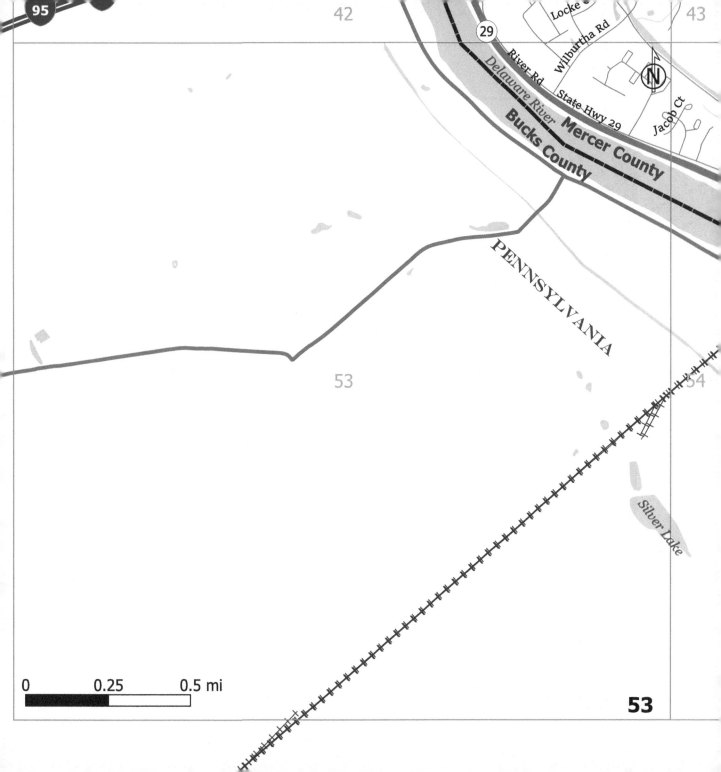

95

29

Locke

Wilburtha Rd

River Rd

State Hwy 29

Jacob Ct

N

Delaware River

Mercer County

Bucks County

PENNSYLVANIA

53

Silver Lake

0   0.25   0.5 mi

53

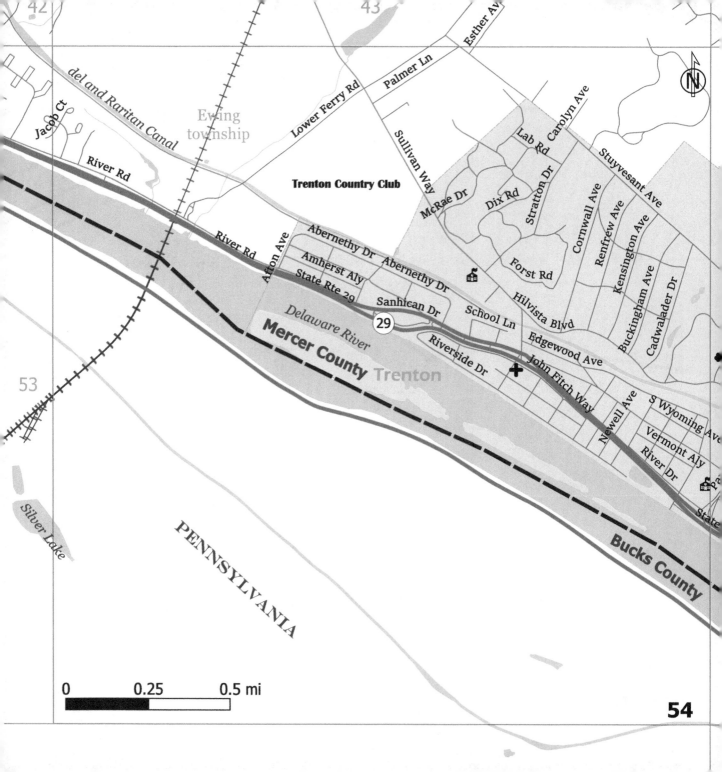

42

43

del and Raritan Canal

Jacob Ct

River Rd

Ewing township

Lower Ferry Rd

Palmer Ln

Esther Ave

Sullivan Way

Trenton Country Club

Lab Rd

Carolyn Ave

Stuyvesant Ave

McRae Dr

Dix Rd

Stratton Dr

Cornwall Ave

Renfrew Ave

Kensington Ave

Buckingham Ave

Cadwalader Dr

River Rd

Afton Ave

Abernethy Dr

Abernethy Dr

Forst Rd

Amherst Aly

State Rte 29

Sanhican Dr

School Ln

Hilvista Blvd

Delaware River

29

Riverside Dr

Edgewood Ave

John Fitch Way

Mercer County

Trenton

Newell Ave

S Wyoming Ave

Vermont Aly

River Dr

State

53

Silver Lake

PENNSYLVANIA

Bucks County

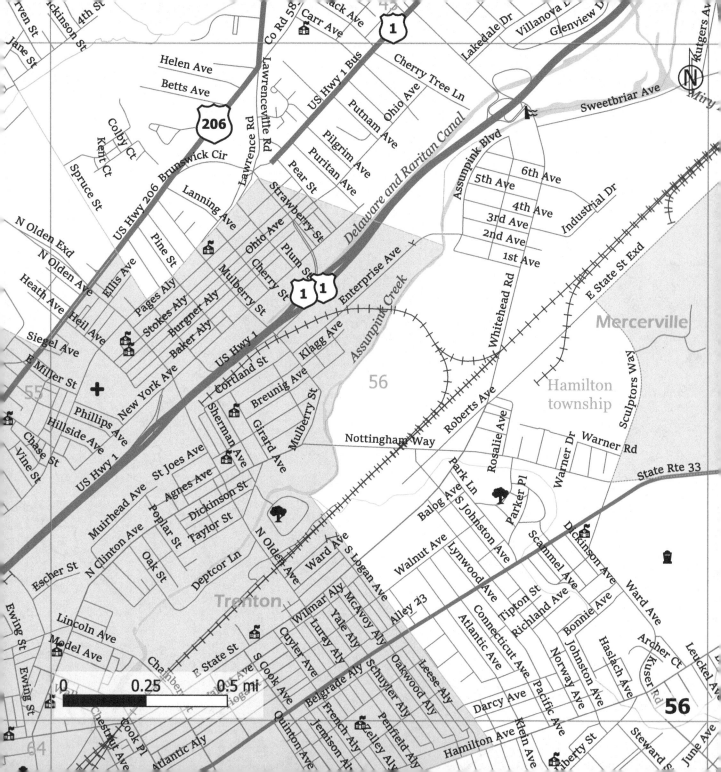

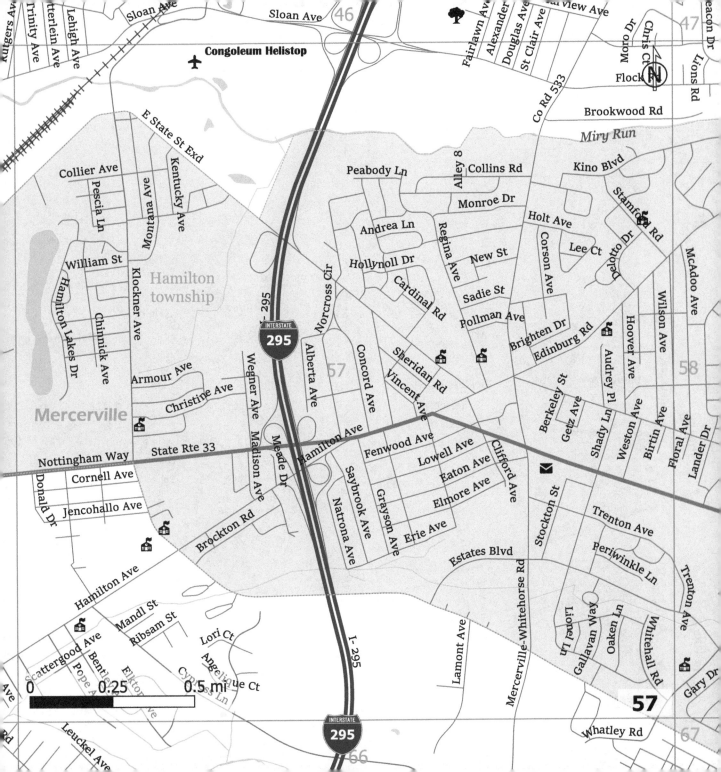

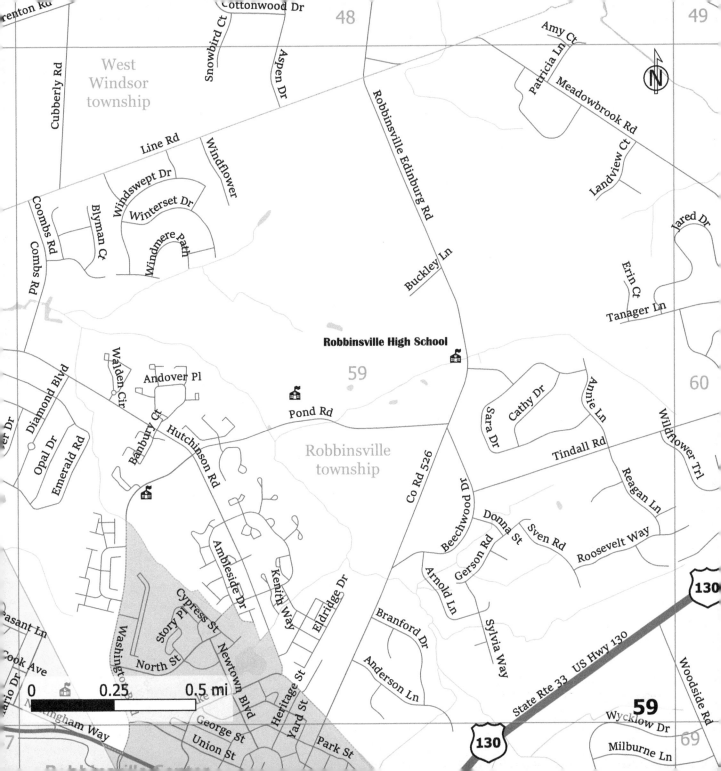

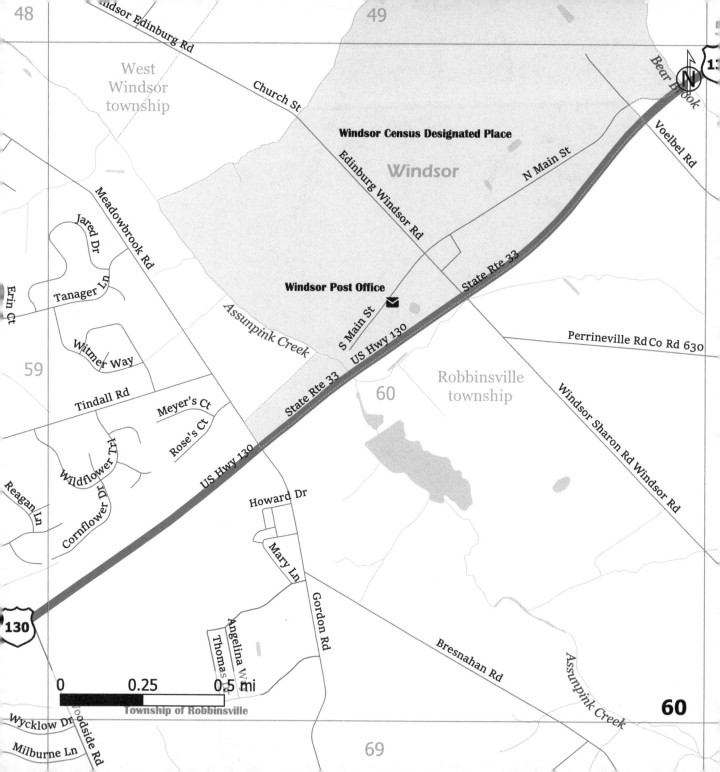

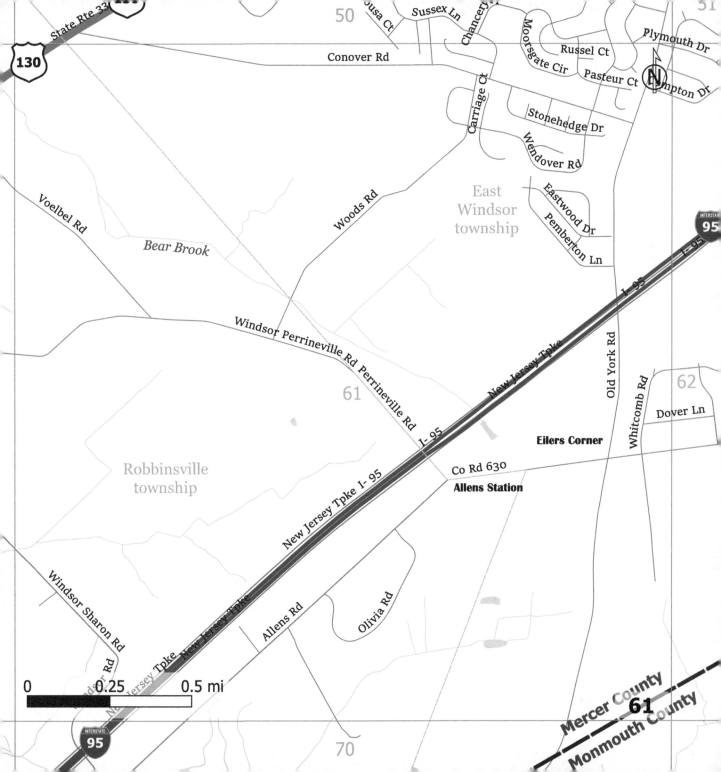

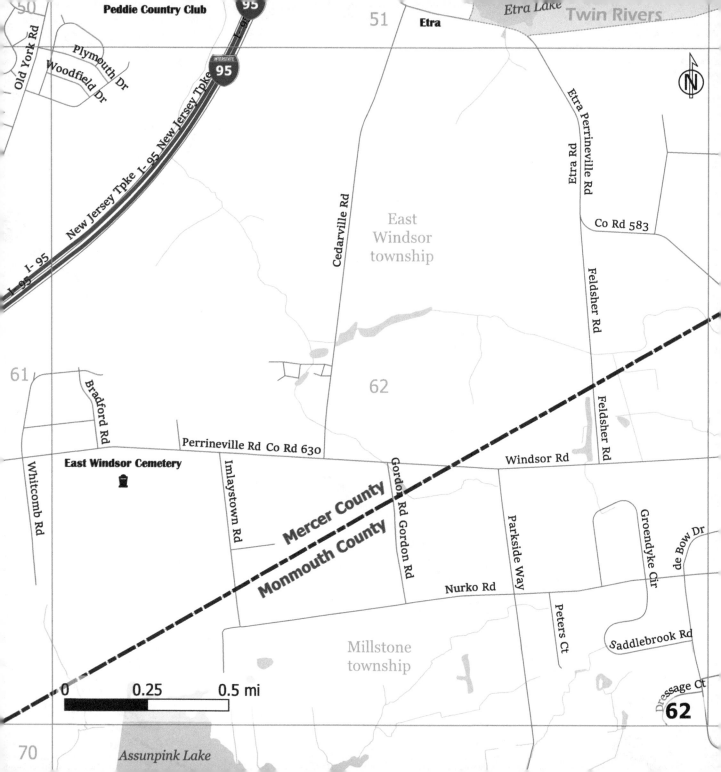

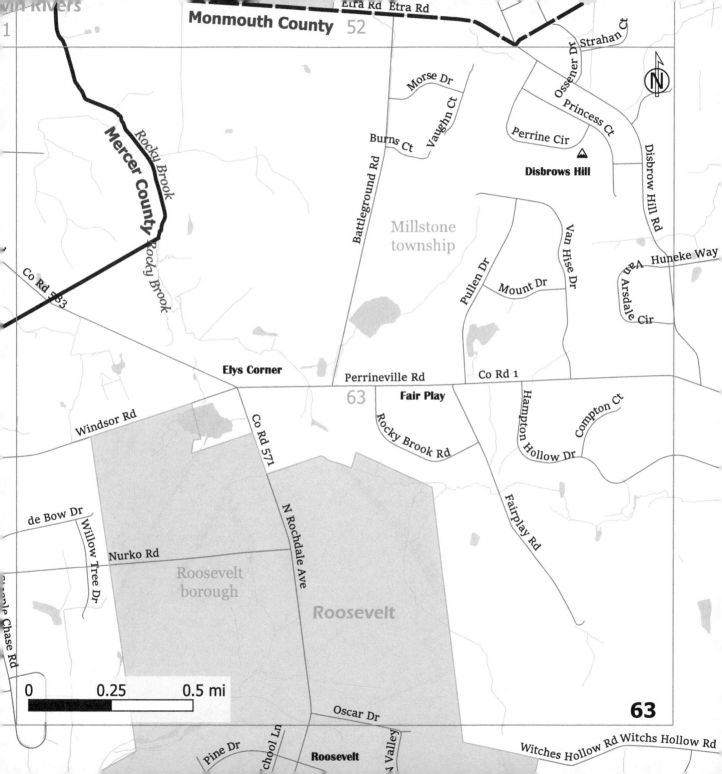

win-Rivers

1

Etra Rd Etra Rd

Strahan Ct

Ossener Dr

Morse Dr

Princess Ct

Vaughn Ct

Perrine Cir

Burns Ct

Battleground Rd

Disbrows Hill

Rocky Brook

Mercer County

Disbrow Hill Rd

Millstone township

Van Hise Dr

Huneke Way

Rocky Brook

Pullen Dr

Mount Dr

Van Arsdale Cir

Co Rd 583

Elys Corner

Perrineville Rd

Co Rd 1

63

Fair Play

Windsor Rd

Co Rd 571

Rocky Brook Rd

Hampton Hollow Dr

Compton Ct

de Bow Dr

Willow Tree Dr

Nurko Rd

N Rochdale Ave

Roosevelt borough

Roosevelt

Fairplay Rd

Dale Chase Rd

0   0.25   0.5 mi

Oscar Dr

Pine Dr

chool Ln

N Valley

Roosevelt

Witches Hollow Rd Witchs Hollow Rd

63

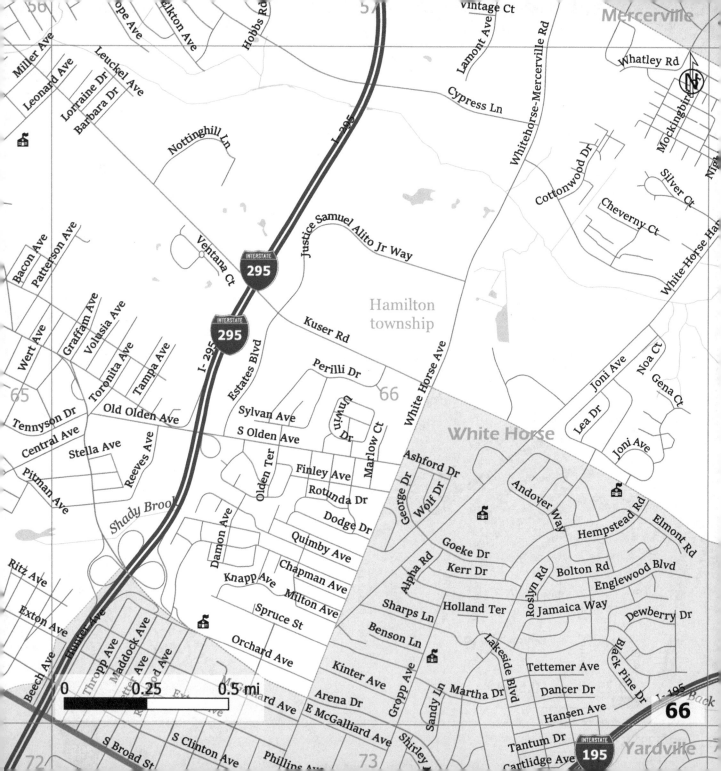

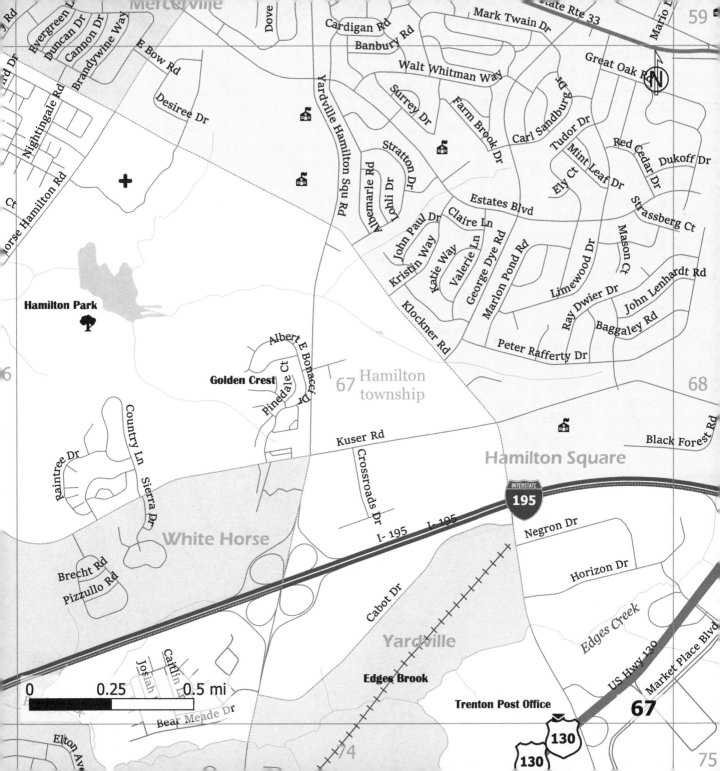

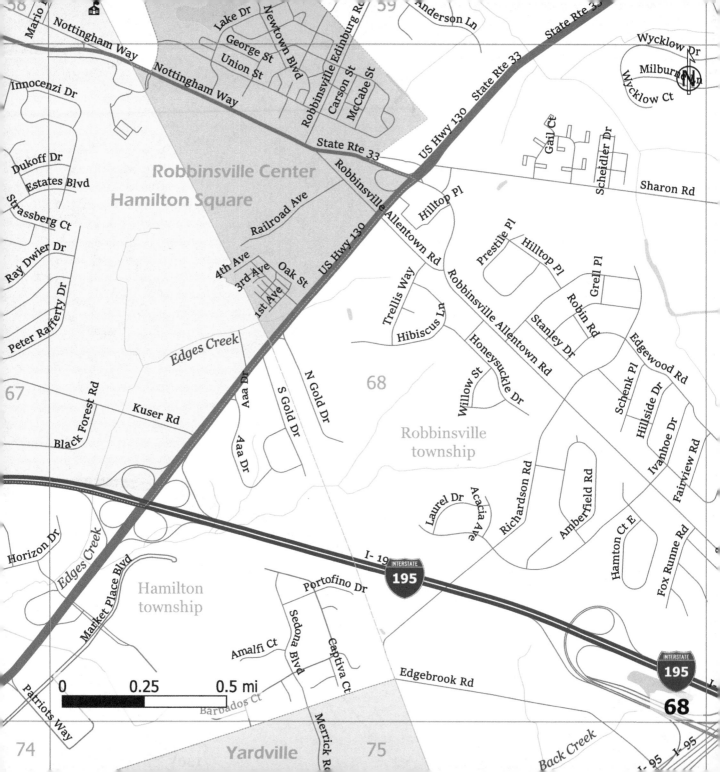

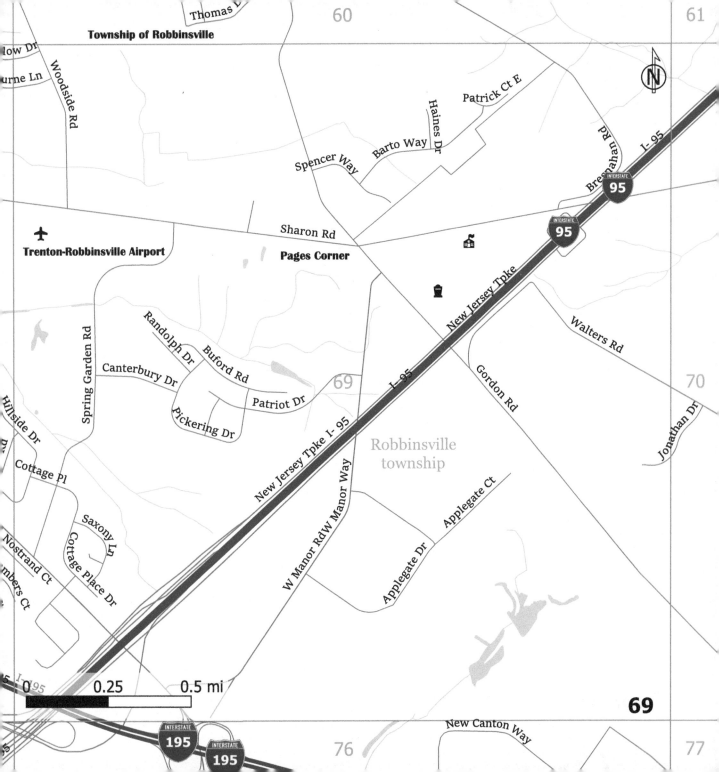

Thomas D

low Dr

urne Ln

Woodside Rd

Township of Robbinsville

Patrick Ct E

Haines Dr

Barto Way

Spencer Way

Breslahan Rd

I- 95

N

INTERSTATE
95

INTERSTATE
95

Sharon Rd

Pages Corner

Trenton-Robbinsville Airport

New Jersey Tpke

Walters Rd

Spring Garden Rd

Randolph Dr

Buford Rd

Canterbury Dr

Patriot Dr

Pickering Dr

I- 95

Gordon Rd

Jonathan Dr

Hillside Dr

Cottage Pl

Robbinsville township

New Jersey Tpke I- 95

W Manor RdW Manor Way

Applegate Ct

Saxony Ln

Cottage Place Dr

Nostrand Ct

mbers Ct

Applegate Dr

Applegate Ct

I- 95

0.25   0.5 mi

69

INTERSTATE
195

INTERSTATE
195

New Canton Way

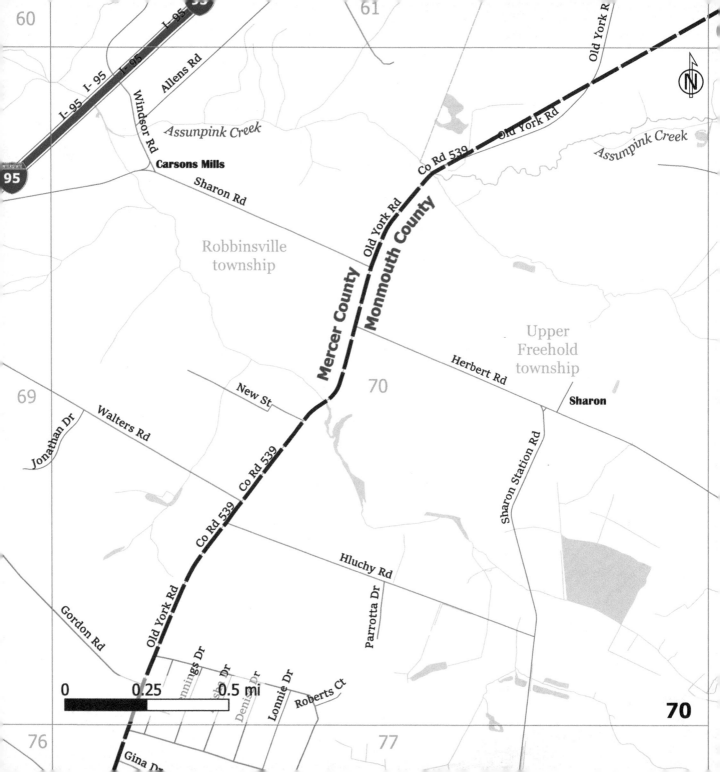

60

61

I-95 33

I-95 I-95 I-95

Allens Rd

Windsor Rd

Assunpink Creek

Carsons Mills

Sharon Rd

INTERSTATE
95

Old York Rd

Old York R

Old York Rd

Co Rd 539

Assunpink Creek

Robbinsville
township

Mercer County

Monmouth County

Old York Rd

70

Upper
Freehold
township

Herbert Rd

69

New St

Jonathan Dr

Walters Rd

Sharon

Sharon Station Rd

Co Rd 539

Co Rd 539

Hluchy Rd

Gordon Rd

Old York Rd

Parrotta Dr

Jennings Dr

Denise Dr

Lonnie Dr

Roberts Ct

0   0.25   0.5 mi

70

76

77

Gina Dr

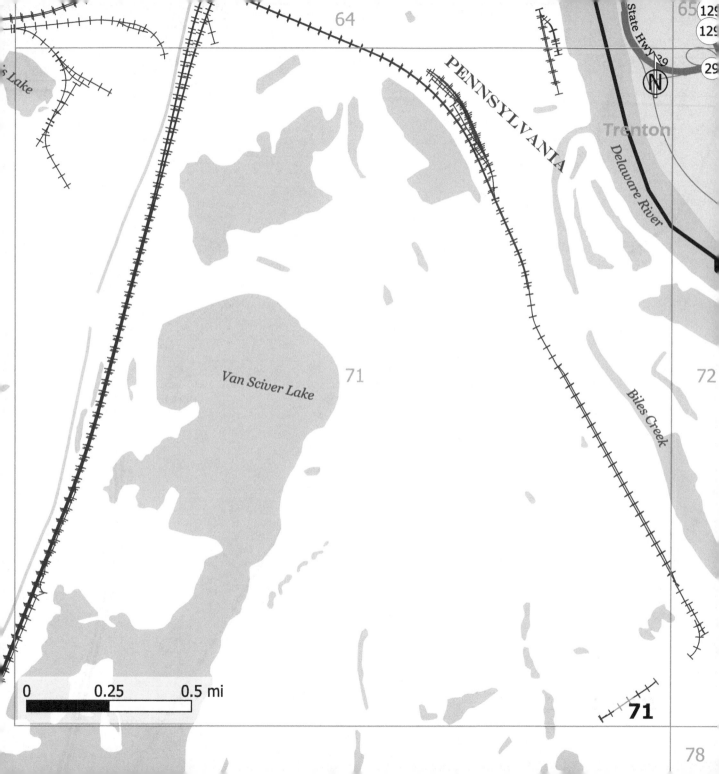

129
129
29

PENNSYLVANIA

N

Trenton

's Lake

Delaware River

Van Sciver Lake

Biles Creek

State Hwy 29

| 0 | 0.25 | 0.5 mi |

71

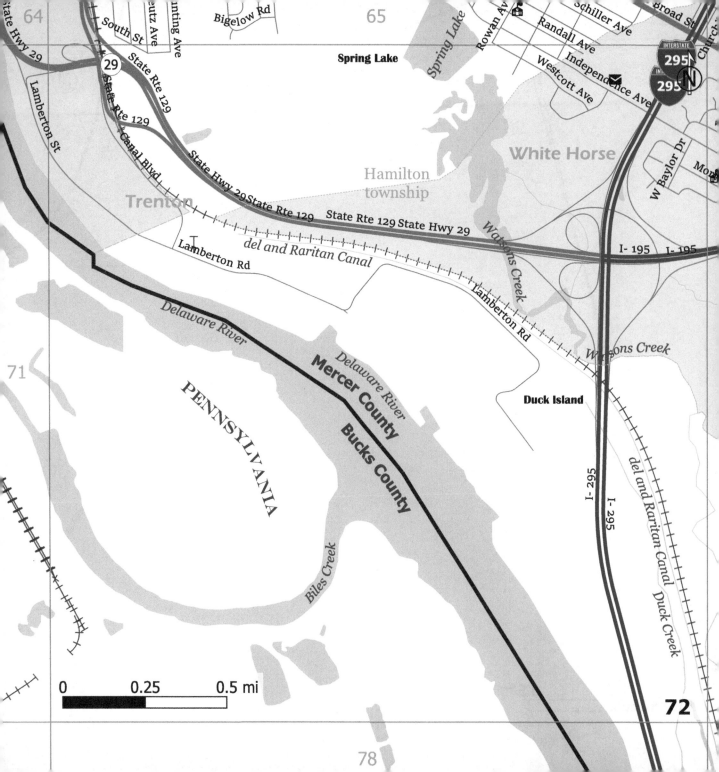

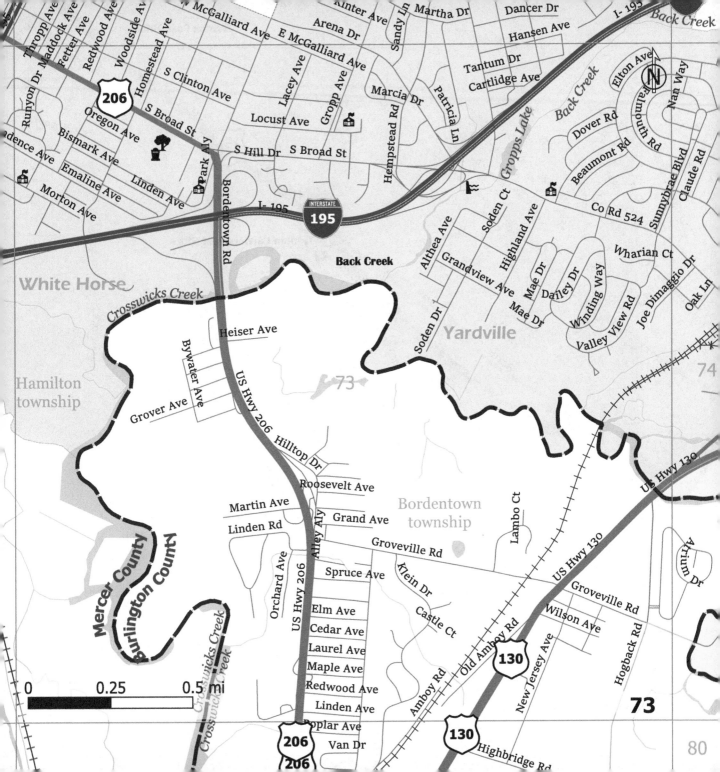

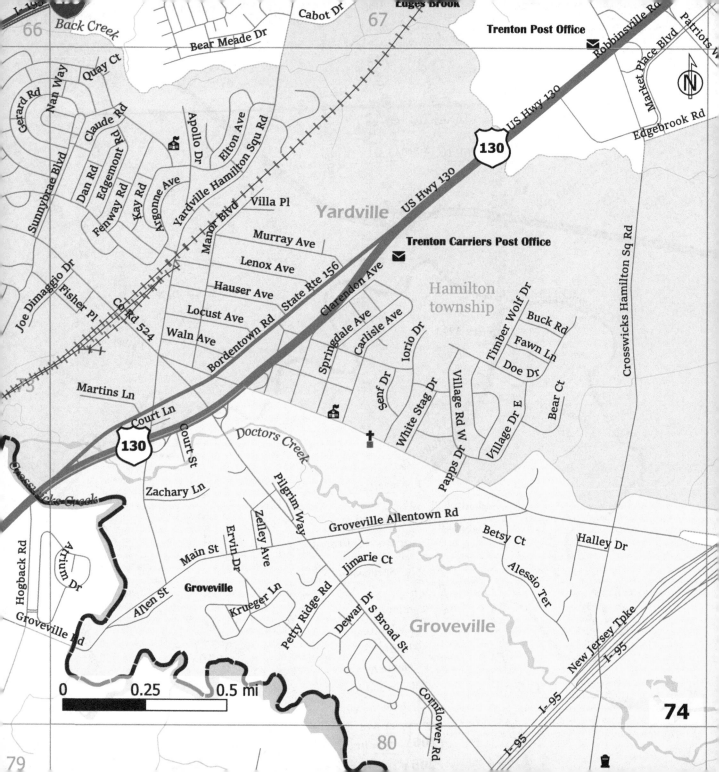

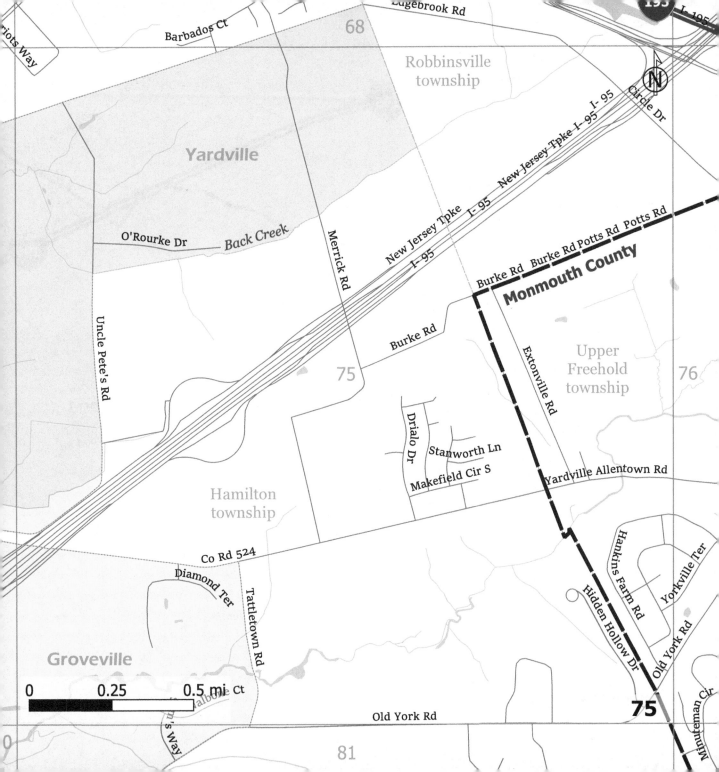

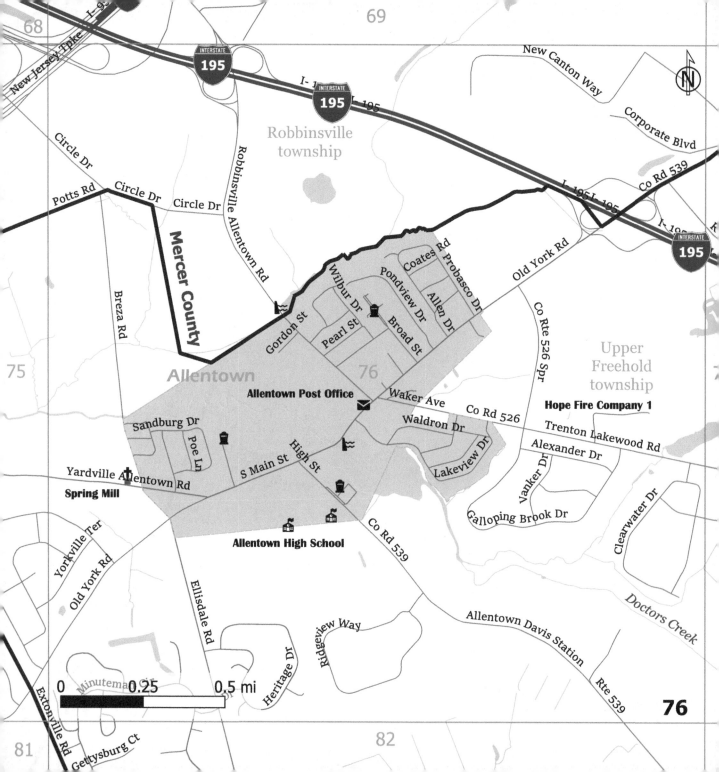

68

69

New Jersey Tpke   I-9

INTERSTATE 195

I-195 INTERSTATE 195

N

New Canton Way

Corporate Blvd

Circle Dr

Potts Rd   Circle Dr   Circle Dr

Robbinsville township

I-195 I-195

Co Rd 539

Mercer County

Robbinsville Allentown Rd

I-195

INTERSTATE 195

Breza Rd

Wilbur Dr

Coates Rd

Probasco Dr

Old York Rd

75

Gordon St

Pearl St

Pondview Dr

Allen Dr

Broad St

Co Rte 526 Spr

Upper Freehold township

Allentown

76

Allentown Post Office

Waker Ave

Co Rd 526

Hope Fire Company 1

Sandburg Dr

Poe Ln

Waldron Dr

Trenton Lakewood Rd

Yardville Allentown Rd

S Main St

High St

Lakeview Dr

Alexander Dr

Vanker Dr

Clearwater Dr

Spring Mill

Co Rd 539

Galloping Brook Dr

Yorkville Ter

Old York Rd

Ellisdale Rd

Allentown High School

Ridgeview Way

Heritage Dr

Allentown Davis Station

Rte 539

Doctors Creek

0   0.25   0.5 mi

Minuteman Cir

Extonville Rd

Gettysburg Ct

76

81

82

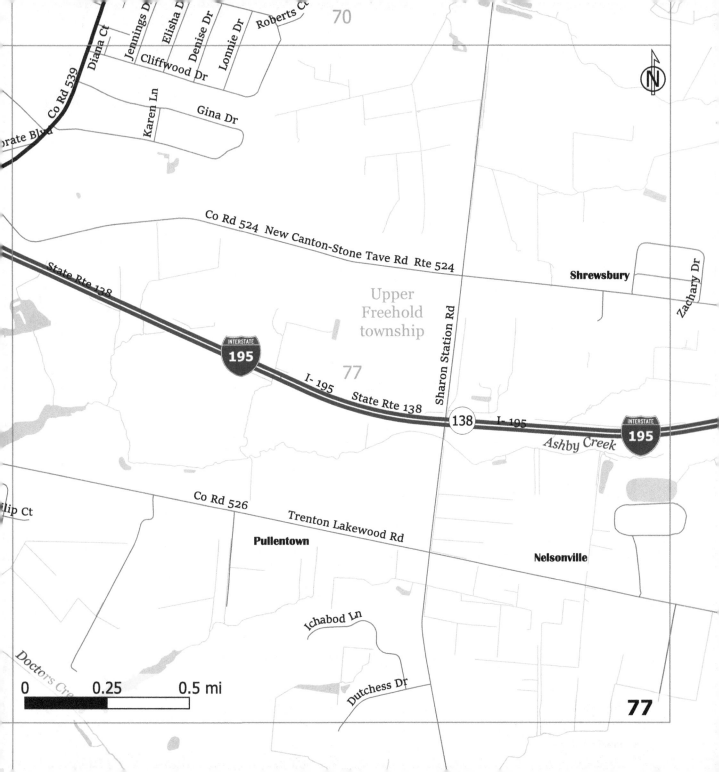

Diana Ct

Jennings D

Elisha D

Denise Dr

Lonnie Dr

Roberts C

Co Rd 539

Cliffwood Dr

rate Blvd

Karen Ln

Gina Dr

Co Rd 524 New Canton-Stone Tave Rd Rte 524

Shrewsbury

Zachary Dr

State Rte 138

Upper
Freehold
township

Sharon Station Rd

INTERSTATE
195

77

I- 195

State Rte 138

138

I- 195

INTERSTATE
195

Ashby Creek

N

Co Rd 526

lip Ct

Trenton Lakewood Rd

Pullentown

Nelsonville

Ichabod Ln

Doctors Cre

0   0.25   0.5 mi

Dutchess Dr

71

72

Duck Creek

INTERSTATE
295

Delaware River

I-295

Mercer County

Delaware River

295

INTERSTATE
295

Crosswicks Cr

PENNSYLVANIA

78

Bucks County

Bordento

Burlington County

Delaware River

W Burlington St

INTERSTATE
295

I-295

S Front St
N Front St

N 2nd St

Fields Aly

3rd St

W Burlington St

Union St

Bordentown
township

78

Burlington St

5th St

Rising Sun R

Lockwood Ave

130

Fieldsboro

0   0.25   0.5 mi

hannel

Newbold Channel

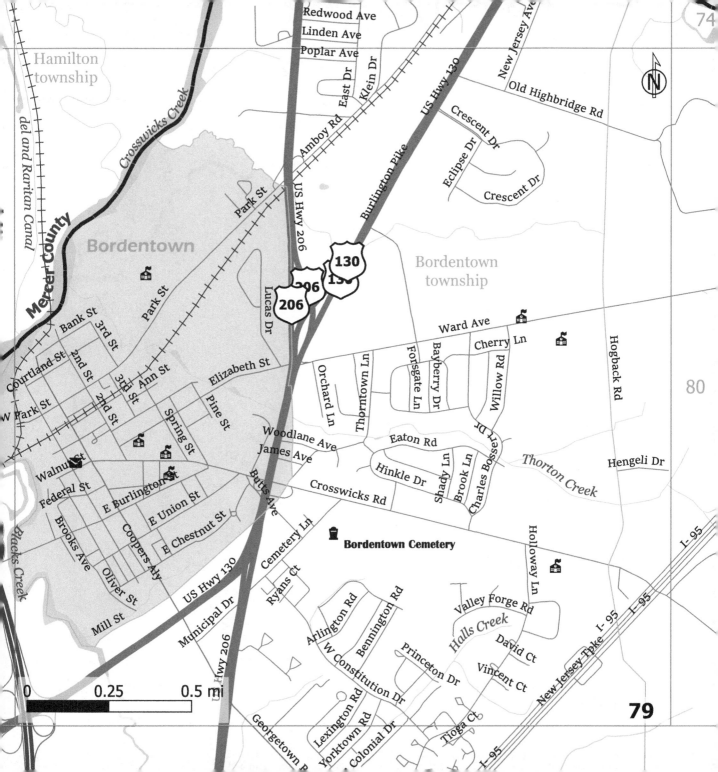

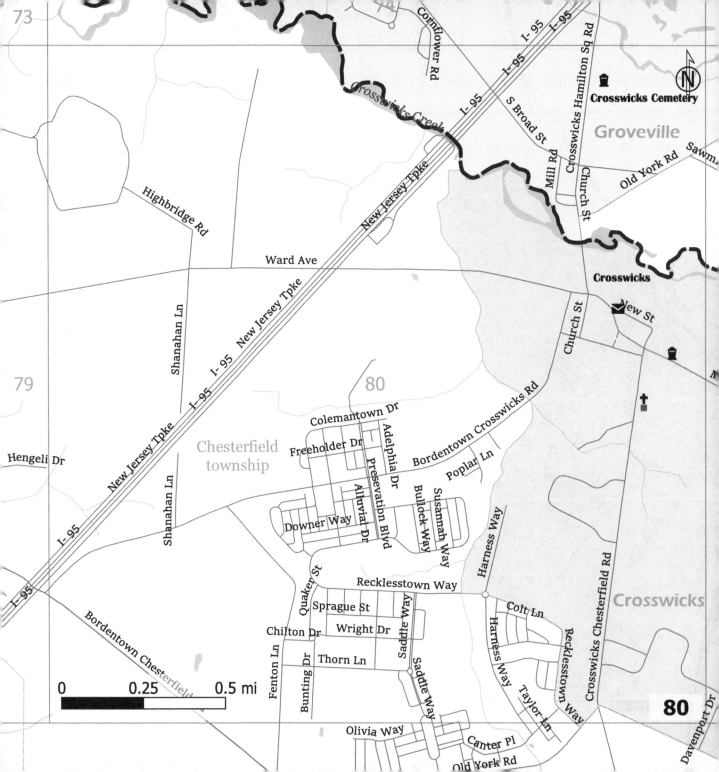

73

Cornflower Rd

I-95

I-95

Crosswicks Hamilton Sq Rd

N

Crosswicks Cemetery

Groveville

Crosswicks Creek

S Broad St

Mill Rd

Church St

Old York Rd

Sawm

Highbridge Rd

New Jersey Tpke

Crosswicks

Ward Ave

Church St

New St

79

80

Shanahan Ln

I-95 New Jersey Tpke

Chesterfield township

Colemantown Dr

Bordentown Crosswicks Rd

Hengeli Dr

Freeholder Dr

Adelphia Dr

Poplar Ln

Preservation Blvd

Shanahan Ln

Alluvial Dr

Susannah Way

Bullock Way

Downer Way

Harness Way

New Jersey Tpke

Quaker St

Recklesstown Way

Crosswicks

I-95

Sprague St

Saddle Way

Colt Ln

Crosswicks Chesterfield Rd

Chilton Dr

Wright Dr

Harness Way

Recklesstown Way

Bordentown Chesterfield

Fenton Ln

Bunting Dr

Thorn Ln

Saddle Way

Taylor Ln

0   0.25   0.5 mi

80

Olivia Way

Canter Pl

Davenport Dr

Old York Rd

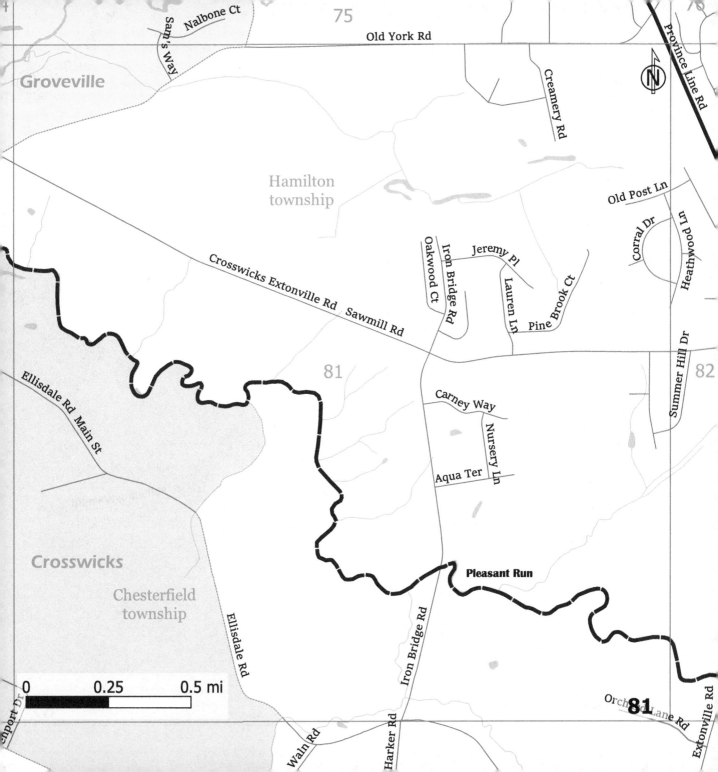

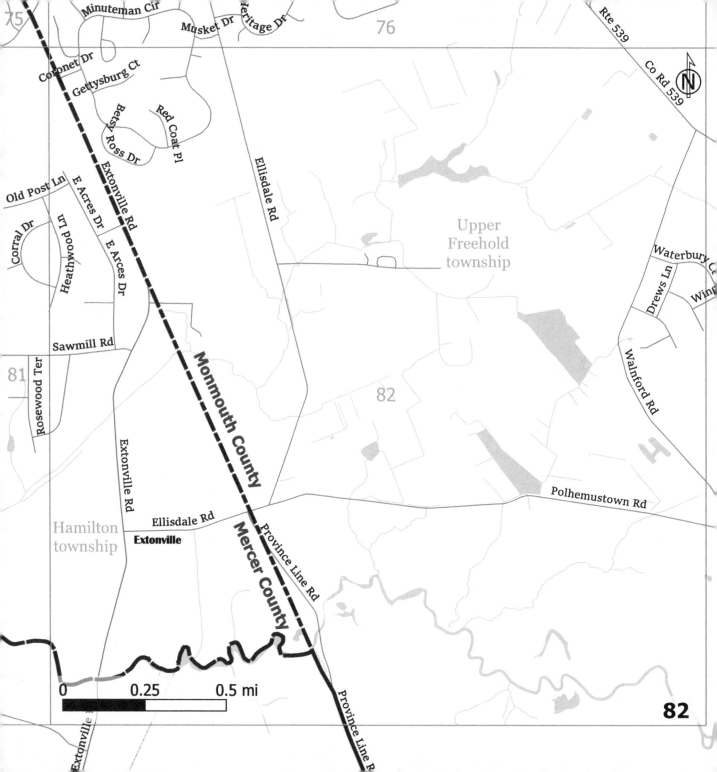

Minuteman Cir

Musket Dr

Heritage Dr

Rte 539

Co Rd 539

N

Coronet Dr

Gettysburg Ct

Betsy Ross Dr

Red Coat Pl

Ellisdale Rd

Upper
Freehold
township

Waterbury C

Old Post Ln

E Acres Dr

Extonville Rd

Drews Ln

Wing

Corral Dr

Heathwood Ln

E Arces Dr

Walnford Rd

Sawmill Rd

Rosewood Ter

Monmouth County

82

Extonville Rd

Polhemustown Rd

Hamilton
township

Ellisdale Rd

Extonville

Mercer County

Province Line Rd

0   0.25   0.5 mi

Extonville R

Province Line R

Made in the USA
Coppell, TX
03 April 2023